A Light Unto Y

Self Discovery Through Investigation of Experience

Pointers to Awakening

Based on the Meditations,
Investigations, Contemplations and Experiences
of Forty Years of Spiritual Search and Practice
By Colin Drake

Revelations Cafe
112 N Main St
Fairfield, IA 52556
641-472-6733

Copyright © 2011 by Colin Drake

Second Edition

ISBN 978-1-105-94517-5

All rights reserved. No part of this book shall be reproduced or transmitted, for commercial purposes, without written permission from the author.

Published by Beyond Awakening Publications, Tomewin

Cover design and photography by the author.

Also by the same author:

Beyond the Separate Self
The End of Anxiety and Mental Suffering

Awareness of Awareness – The Open Way

Awakening and Beyond
Self-Recognition and its Consequences

Poetry From Beyond The Separate Self

Poetry From Being A Light Unto The Self

Humanity Our Place in the Universe
The Central Beliefs of the Worlds Religions

Poetry From Awakening and Beyond

Poetry From Awareness of Awareness

All of these titles are available as: e-books and in hard copy at
http://www.lulu.com/spotlight/ColinDrake

Contents

Introduction	4
Prologue – The Problem	21
1 Each Moment Reveals the Absolute	29
2 A Light unto Yourself	37
3 Separation is Suffering	44
4 Awakening	47
5 The Myth of Doing Nothing	52
6 Restless Mind … No Problem	58
7 Memories are Made of This	67
8 Nonduality	72
9 Awakening is not an Experience	77
10 Awareness a No-Brainer	83
11 The Fundamental Secret	89
12 Awareness of Awareness	96
13 Hakuin's Song of Freedom	102
14 Investigation is Experiential not Intellectual	106
15 Nonduality and Religion	113
16 Instruments of the Absolute	120
17 Purpose and Meaning	126
18 On This and That	143
19 Nothing Has Essential Meaning	150
20 Free Will … Myth or Reality?	159
21 The Practical Application of Awakening	167
22 Love: Agape and Eros	174
Appendix One: So What … What Now?	192
Appendix Two: All or Nothing	203
Spiritual Biography	209
Glossary	212
Index	214
Bibliography	221

Introduction

Introduction

The aim of this book is twofold: firstly to help you, the reader, become 'a light unto yourself'. This will be facilitated by providing a framework in which you can investigate the nature of your moment to moment experience, which hopefully will result in you achieving what the Buddha called 'the first factor of enlightenment': becoming 'aware of awareness'. The second is to provide pointers so that the book can help shed 'light onto your Self'. That is to point to the nature of your true Self, which can be discovered by your own investigations.

This book is the sequel to *Beyond the Separate Self* (hereafter called *Beyond*) and is a collection of articles written since this was published. These are mainly of two types: the first being replies to questions, comments and criticisms from readers of the book; and the second being the outcome of my ongoing investigations.

I carry out these investigations to deepen my own understanding of the nature of Reality and then write them down when new insights arise. This is so that I can re-read

Introduction

them and then continue my investigation from any of these 'staging points' that have been discovered. Some of these insights are so subtle, and tenuous, that they are easily buried by day-to-day living. It's rather like exploring a trackless wilderness in stages and adding to the 'map' after each exploration.

However, these additions are rare and most investigation involves re-covering mapped ground. Moreover, even this is very useful as one 'sees' deeper and discovers nuances that were missed on previous excursions. This deepening entails becoming more established in identifying with and as pure awareness ... which is 'the name of the game'. The continual 'seeing' slowly changes one's psyche and mind-set from identifying with the body/mind to identifying with the deeper level of pure awareness.

Another thing to bear in mind is that the 'map' is not a linear path and that any staging point that has been discovered after one has become 'aware of awareness' may be used as the starting point for further investigation. Rather like being able to dive into the ocean from a variety of locations. Now I can use any of the discoveries that I have made as a springboard

Introduction

from which to re-commence the exploration. The wonderful thing is that there is no end to this investigation as what is being explored is limitless.

As time goes by you too will make your own discoveries and verbalize your own pathways into this recognition of pure awareness. I strongly advise you to record in writing these discoveries and pathways, as the reading of them before your practice will put you in the right frame of mind, and inspire you. In the final analysis your 'pathway in' will become particular to your own mind, and writings produced by your mind will always appeal more than those produced by another mind. Ultimately you have to become, as the Buddha said, 'a light unto yourself'.

One other point is that the aim is to become completely established in 'awareness of awareness' and identified with pure awareness. For this no effort is required, just relaxing into and recognizing awareness itself. Rather like jumping into the ocean and then floating effortlessly… As this takes place one is carried by the prevailing 'currents' and new insights are encountered spontaneously. If these do not occur

Introduction

this is not a problem as awareness of, and identification with, awareness is the goal.

So these articles were written by me in the spirit of being 'a light unto myself' and it is hoped they will be of some use to you, the reader, in your own investigations. As you follow this 'map' you need to consider each scene (staging point) carefully and see whether you can truly 'see' what is being said. Hopefully when this 'seeing' occurs they will provide staging points from which you can start your own inquiry.

There is necessarily some duplication between them as what is being discussed is so simple. They are different 'takes' on the same simplicity, presenting the material in various ways whilst building upon what has been discovered, so some repetition is unavoidable. It should also be noted that each of these are, as far as is possible, stand-alone investigations/contemplations, or answers to readers, thus they need to make sense by themselves. Therefore some sections of each will contain similar passages, so that they are relatively complete when read in isolation.

Introduction

This duplication can in fact be very valuable for it is not enough to become 'aware of awareness' once and assume that this will produce profound awakening. This seeing is an awakened moment which will soon tend to be submerged by old thought patterns. To overcome these requires experiencing these awakened moments regularly on a daily (hourly, or minutely would be better) basis. That is why I recommend relaxing into the recognition of pure awareness at least three times daily ... see *'So What ... What Now?'* in the appendix.

To aid this process the basic eight steps of investigation which reveal that we are awareness itself (and that everything arises in, exists in and subsides back into this) are repeated at the beginning, middle and end of the book in the first, eleventh and twenty first chapters. Every time I use this process myself I find it grows in power as these steps become more obvious. Even now ten years after they were developed I still use them occasionally to deepen my identification with awareness.

It's rather like having a disease and being given a course of antibiotics and pain-killers. It's not enough to take the medication once and feel much better, one must continue until the course of medication has been finished and the disease is

Introduction

completely cured. In the same way, for most of us, the disease of misidentification with the body/mind is chronic, having been established as long as we can remember and to cure it completely is going to require a prolonged course of treatment.

However, in the same way that each pain-killer relieves the symptoms of a physical disease, so each investigation and discovery of awareness will relieve the symptoms of misidentification. Also as one takes more pain killers when the symptoms return, so when mental suffering and anxiety (the symptoms of misidentification) return these can be dispelled by becoming 'aware of awareness' and re-identifying with this.

This brings up a very important point: any time where there is any mental suffering caused by identifying with painful thoughts, or feelings, this should be a wake-up call to the fact that we are misidentifying. Any mental suffering can be used as a direct pointer back to the deeper level of our being: pure awareness.

As the chapters of this book build upon what has been discussed in *Beyond* many of them contain portions of that

Introduction

work. The focus of that was self-identity, which has been broadened in this present work to include other aspects of Reality. This book also contains more practical information with regard to enhancing one's own investigations and living in the world... *Beyond* also contained such pointers which sometimes just needed rearranging to inform the topic under consideration.

It could be argued that I should have reworded these sections to avoid repetition. However, as these were all written spontaneously as a direct result of my inquiries/contemplations they would lose some of their directness and aliveness if they were changed. I have come across teachers who are continually rewording their message in an attempt to avoid well worn words and phrases, with the result that what they say gets more and more obscure. It is said that 'the Tao cannot be spoken', which is true, but there are words which point to it quite clearly. When you abandon words such as awareness, The Absolute, enlightenment, awakening, emptiness, nothingness etc. the message becomes very 'muddy' and almost unintelligible.

Introduction

Each chapter should be treated as an aid to your enquiry into the nature of Reality, and as such should not just be read and intellectually considered but need to be taken slowly, step by step, not moving onto the next step until one fully 'sees' the step that is being considered. This does not mean to say that one needs to agree with each statement, as any investigation is personal, but one needs to understand what is being said. Also to get the most out of each chapter one needs to spend some time contemplating it until one 'feels' what it is pointing to; if a chapter is just read without due attention then its significance may well be missed.

The prologue describes, clearly and succinctly, the problem with misidentifying as a separate object and the need to overcome this. It also sets the scene for the chapters that follow. This is an edited version of chapter one of *Beyond The Separate Self* and, as such, may be skipped over by its readers if they wish.

Chapter one is a result of a recent contemplation into my direct experience of the moment and quickly morphed into investigating the properties of the Absolute. When I came to write this down I found I could do no better than use sections

Introduction

of writings resulting from other contemplations. However, this was very useful as I had decided to start this book by recapping the basic framework for investigating one's moment to moment experience, and when I reread the finished article it had done just that ... plus a bit more!

Chapter two was the reply to a reader who compared *Beyond* with teachings he had acquired from *A Course in Miracles*. The gist of the response is that the initial investigation of experience must be carried out from a position of 'knowing nothing'. Then one's discoveries are one's own, not second hand, and if the process is pursued one becomes 'a light unto oneself'.

Chapter three was the outcome of my own mental suffering caused by re-identifying myself as an object ... an old habit my mind occasionally relapses into. I decided to really stick it to my mind by putting together a punchy article to which I could refer whenever this old habit resurfaced. This brings up the point that I write these articles for myself as much as for others. They are a case in point of me being 'a light unto myself'.

Introduction

Chapter four resulted from a contemplation concerning who indeed is the experiencer? What is it that has always been present and has witnessed my entire life? The investigation took a slightly different, and much more direct, route than is often the case. The results are then confirmed by agreeing with passages from the Upanishads. However, such confirmation is useless unless the results are the outcome of one's own experiential investigations.

Chapter five was inspired by a friend who had been interested in nonduality, reading books and attending satsangs, for many years but who still suffered from acute existential anxiety. However, when questioned it turned out that he did nothing, on a regular basis, to establish himself in nondual awareness. He had been greatly influenced by teachers who say there is nothing one can do, and that everything just 'happens by itself', but that had just left him with the feeling of complete despair.

Chapter six was the direct result of my own experiences of 'relaxing into awareness' when my mind was very busy or restless. I discovered that this was absolutely not a problem as there is nothing to achieve, find, or get as awareness is always

Introduction

present. This very recognition meant that the restless mind was no longer regarded as an obstacle, and this in turn tended to result in the mind settling by itself. But even if this did not happen it wasn't a problem as awareness is totally unaffected by anything occurring in it.

Chapter seven is my reply to a reader who had read in *Dialogue of Consciousness* that 'memory is just a concept' and that 'nothing exists'. She did not know quite what to make of this evidenced by her query: 'But **sometimes I also wonder if people are still there when I'm not there.**' This chapter is my 'take' on these two earlier statements.

Chapter eight was written in reply to an invitation to define nonduality. I was going to be interviewed on the radio and the first suggested question was 'What is Nonduality?' My reply starts with a definition of nonduality and then relies heavily on chapter four of *Beyond*: 'The Perceiver not the Perceived'. This is because I could not find any way of saying it better ... for me it put it in a nutshell.

Chapter nine was written as a direct response from a reader who said he was longing for the experience of awakening.

Introduction

This very common and I suffered from it for over twenty years. However, awakening is not an experience but a recognition of something that has never been lost, and the experiences that result from this realization are ephemeral and vary greatly from person to person.

Chapter ten is the response to a sceptic materialist who had read one of my articles in a general newsletter. It does address the most common issue, which is that most people think that there cannot be any awareness without a brain. In fact many people hold this as self-evident due to identification with their body/mind. So I was glad to posit that 'awareness is a no-brainer!'

Chapter eleven was my response to the movie *The Secret* which posits that one can gain everything one wants by applying 'the law of attraction'. 'Ask, believe and receive' is the motto of those that wish to create abundance by applying the power of their mind and positive thinking. However, there is a much more fundamental secret by which one realizes that 'absolute abundance' is always present. This only requires a simple recognition and then it is always available.

Introduction

Chapter twelve came about due to the intransigence of one of my readers, with whom I have had a lengthy correspondence, who could not recognise the difference between awareness and thought. I decided to point out as many differences as I could and also to stress the importance of becoming 'aware of awareness'.

Chapter thirteen was the result of my studies during which I encountered the beautiful 'Song of Freedom' by Hakuin. I could see that to fully appreciate this one needed to understand key Buddhist terms so I decided to write a commentary on it. These terms are also defined in the glossary.

Chapter fourteen was a direct response to someone who said they had realized pure awareness but this had not banished their anxiety. This is because this realization was intellectual, rather than experiential; or because they had not cultivated this realization until it was firmly established. This chapter elaborates on these issues.

Chapter fifteen was stimulated by the comments of one of the keynote speakers at a nonduality conference. He posited that spirituality is breaking away from religion. However,

Introduction

spirituality (and, up to a point, nonduality) are basic to all of the major religions, so I felt the balance needed to be redressed.

Chapter sixteen is a result of my own investigations and contemplations into the function of conscious beings. For this to be experiential I had to start with my own body/mind and then extrapolate the results as applying to all conscious organisms. I also consider how the world's religions see this and show how the Upanishads concur with my findings.

Chapter seventeen is a combination of the chapter in *Beyond* on 'Purpose and Meaning' and a more exhaustive essay, on the same subject, that I wrote as a major assignment for a philosophy unit. The main difference is that this new article is deeper and distinguishes between purpose and meaning.

Chapter eighteen is an updated version of 'On This and That', the poem that appears in *Beyond.* It clarifies a few points in the original, and has been provided with a more extensive commentary. The purpose of the poem is that it is short, easy to remember, and is a précis of just about everything I have discovered!

Introduction

Chapter nineteen investigates whether anything has essential meaning. That is whether any 'thing' has meaning with regard to our essential identity, who or what we are. It also addresses the major human problem of 'reading meaning into things that have no meaning' In addition there is a discussion about the essential meaning of nothingness.

Chapter twenty is my response to a teacher who is a determinist, which means that he believes that we have no free will at all. At the Absolute level this is clear, for there is no personal self and therefore no personal free will ... only the will of the Absolute. At the surface level of mind/body this is less clear and this chapter explores this.

Chapter twenty one came about when my neighbour asked me for help in achieving equanimity whist beset with worldly troubles. I realized that, although I had sympathy for his plight, this would not help him at all. What was required was a paradigm shift so that he could respond to his worldly problems in a spontaneous and therefore appropriate (for him) manner, rather than to react to them.

Introduction

Chapter twenty two is an adapted essay from my honours degree, which considered the differences between Eros, a form of individual love, and Agape, universal love. It attempts to show that the former is exhibited by those who identify themselves as 'separate beings', and the latter by those identify themselves with the universal – the Totality of consciousness and energy.

Wrapping up the book posed me a problem for I was looking for a way to finish by offering practical pointers on how to become fully established in 'awareness of awareness', that is identification with and as pure awareness, whilst living one's day to day worldly life. So I decided to add appendices consisting of two vital chapters from *Beyond* which contain this information. I took this approach as I found I could do no better than repeating 'So What … What Now?' and 'All or Nothing'. They are my own set of practical suggestions and I find them as fresh and helpful as ever when I read them, so I offer no apology for including them. They are yet another example of me being 'a light unto myself'.

They also make this book 'complete' in itself so that it does not rely on the reader owning a copy of *Beyond*, although for

Introduction

going completely *Beyond the Separate Self* this would be beneficial. If you have any questions or would like to leave feedback you are welcome to e-mail me at colin108@dodo.com.au . I am quite happy to clarify any points that you do not understand; however, I would rather not field questions on topics that are clearly covered in the text. If you are not sure it would be advisable to wait until you have finished the book, as you may well find that your question is answered.

This second edition has been improved by eliminating some needless repetition and by embellishing three chapters with the poems based on them. I write poems on most of my articles which are then published separately and sometimes these add significantly to the original by stressing new facets which had not been previously elucidated. In the case of those I have included in this book I felt this had occurred and am happy to add them to the essays that inspired them.

Prologue

The Problem

A general discussion on the problem of identifying oneself as an individual object in a universe of multiple objects. It also sets the framework for the investigations that follow which reveal a deeper level of being than that of thoughts and sensations. This is an edited version of chapter one of *Beyond The Separate Self* and, as such, may be skipped over by its readers if they wish.

Prologue – The Problem

For most of us much of our waking time is spent in obsessive thinking about 'ourselves' and our relationships with other people. This is especially true when we are not working, using our minds in a productive activity; or when we are not relaxing in such a way that engages the mind such as reading a book, playing a game or watching a screen. For the mind is akin to an onboard-computer which is a wonderful tool for problem-solving, information storing, retrieval and processing, and evaluating the data provided by our senses. However, when it is not fully utilized it tends to search for other problems to solve, and if these are not presently available it tends to speculate about the future, delve into the past, or imagine in the present, creating non-existent problems which it then tries to solve!

Most people tend to identify with their mind, rather than seeing it as a tool, which creates myriad problems. This causes everything to be seen through the filter of the mind: its opinions, judgements, and self-interest. When this happens we cease to see things as they really are which lessens our ability to relate to the world in a natural healthy way. Imagine the problems it would cause if your computer decided that it was 'you' and coloured all the information it retrieved from the internet with its own arbitrary opinions and judgements. In this case you would be unable to rely on any of this information, and if you did then any decisions made using this would be liable to be faulty.

In the above example 'you' are obviously not the computer but the perceiver of the data provided by the computer and all of its multimedia functionality. In the same way, we have a deeper level of being than the mind (thoughts and mental images) and body (physical sensations), which is also the perceiver of this 'data'. However, when we identify at the surface level of mind/body we are unaware of this and tend to suffer due to the shortcomings of our mind/body. This is akin to suffering because our computer is not the most up-to-date, fastest attractive model available.

This is exactly what most of us do, worrying about our body-image and mental capacity and ability. We tend to expand our concept of self-identity to include an imaginary self-image consisting of our physical appearance, mental ability, status, occupation, position in society, family situation, achievements, lack of achievements, ambitions, hopes, fears, memories and projections into the future. Not only do we consider this to be

Prologue – The Problem

who or what we are, and continually obsess about this, but we also spend large periods of time comparing this with the equally erroneous images we have formed of other people we relate to.

So we have identified ourselves as an imaginary object, in a universe of separate objects, which we then compare with other imaginary objects! This is bound to lead to confusion, suffering and an increased feeling of separation, which is exacerbated by the fact that we do not even see these other objects as they actually are, but as we imagine them to be through the filter of our mind's opinions, judgements and self-interest.

To free ourselves from this nightmarish scenario and the continual obsession with the 'separate self' we imagine ourselves to be, we need to connect with the deeper level of our being as the 'subject' rather than an 'object', where we are the perceiver of our thoughts and sensations. This level is ever-present as there is continual awareness of our thoughts and sensations. Whilst we identify with the mind this level is overlooked; the mind continues the vicious circle of obsessive thinking by processing these thoughts and sensations and relating them to the imaginary self-image that it has concocted.

However, we can easily escape from this vicious circle by simply investigating the nature and relationship of these thoughts and sensations and our awareness of them. When this is fully accomplished we discover that, at the deepest level, we are the perceiver of these thoughts and sensations. These are just ephemeral objects which come and go, leaving the perceiver totally unaffected, in the same way that the sky is unaffected by the clouds which scud across it, or the ocean is undisturbed by the waves and swells that appear on its surface.

This is what this book is designed to achieve, to take one beyond the 'separate self' we have imagined ourselves to be. In this we discover that most of our worries have no foundation for they are just the mind projecting into the future, wallowing in the past, or obsessing over the imaginary self-image it has conjured up. Once the mind is put in its place – as the servant and not the master – we start to see things as they truly are, and to recognize not only the deeper level of being within ourselves but also to recognize this in those around us. Then we see that our self-image and the images we have created of other people are all just illusions. At this deeper level we relate to others in a much more loving, wholesome way, for it becomes clear that there is in fact no separation between ourselves and others, as at this level we share the same constant conscious subjective presence.

This is not a question of belief or imagination but of discovery by direct investigation, and for this to be effective we need to put aside all belief systems and acquired knowledge concerning who we are at the underlying level beyond thoughts and sensations. The only knowledge of this that is valid is that which is revealed to each one of us by direct experience. The easiest way for this direct experience to occur is by enquiring into the nature of experience itself, and for this enquiry to be effective we need to start from the position of believing and knowing nothing.

Before starting we need to discuss the nature of awareness itself. It is obvious that we would not 'know' (be aware of) our own perceptions without awareness being present. This does not mean that we are always conscious of each one of them, as this is dictated by where we put our attention, or upon what we focus our mind. However, all sensations detected by the body are there in awareness, and we can readily become conscious of them by turning our attention to them. It is also true that our thoughts and mental images immediately appear in awareness, but these require less attention to be seen as they occur in the mind itself. So awareness is like the screen on which all of our thoughts and sensations appear, and the mind becomes conscious of these by focusing on them. Take, for example, what happens when you open your eyes and look at a beautiful view: everything seen immediately appears in awareness, but for the mind to make anything of this it needs to focus upon certain elements of what is seen. 'There is an amazing tree', 'wow look at that eagle', 'what a stunning sky', etc. To be sure, you may just make a statement like 'what a beautiful view', but this does not in itself say much and is so self-evident as to be not worth saying!

The point is that the mind is a tool for problem-solving, information storing, retrieval and processing, and evaluating the data provided by our senses. It achieves this by focusing on specific sensations, thoughts or mental images that are present in awareness, and 'processing' these. In fact we only truly see 'things as they are' when they are not seen through the filter of the mind, and this occurs when what is encountered is able to 'stop the mind'. For instance we have all had glimpses of this at various times in our lives, often when seeing a beautiful sunset, a waterfall or some other wonderful natural phenomenon. These may seem other-worldly or intensely vivid, until the mind kicks in with any evaluation when everything seems to return to 'normal'. In fact nature is much more vivid and alive when directly perceived, and the more we identify with the 'perceiver', as awareness itself, the more frequently we see things 'as they are'.

The following chapters are aids in the investigation of one's moment-to-moment experience. These are designed to enable you to discover this deeper level of being where you are truly the 'perceiver' not the 'perceived'.[1]

---

[1] C. Drake, *Beyond The Separate Self,* 2009, Halifax, p.10-16.

Chapter One

Each Moment Reveals the Absolute

There must be understanding which comes with alert perceptivity, eager enquiry and deep investigation.[2]

An investigation of one's moment to moment existence, which reveals the nature of the Absolute Reality.

---

[2] Nisargadatta, *I Am That*, 1997, Durham NY, p. 534.

Each Moment Reveals the Absolute Reality

Below follows a simple method to investigate the nature of reality starting with one's own moment to moment experience. You need to let go of all pre-conceived ideas of who, or what, you 'are' and start from a position of 'knowing nothing'. The investigation need to be carried out in a scientific, experimental, spirit. Each step should be considered until one experiences, or 'sees', its validity before moving on to the following step. That is to say that you should 'test' each one by considering it to see if it corresponds to your own direct experience. If you reach a step where you do not find this possible, continue on regardless in the same way, and hopefully the flow of the investigation will make this step clear. By all means examine each step critically but with an open mind, for if you only look for 'holes' that's all you will find!

Consider the following statement: 'Life, for each of us, is just a series of moment-to-moment experiences'. These experiences start when we are born and continue until we die, rushing headlong after each other, so that they seem to merge into a whole that we call 'my life'. However, if we stop to look we can readily see that, for each of us, every moment is just an experience.

Each Moment Reveals the Absolute

Any moment of experience has only three elements: thoughts (including all mental images), sensations (everything sensed by the body and its sense organs) and awareness of these thoughts and sensations. Emotions and feelings are a combination of thought and sensation.

Thoughts and sensations are ephemeral, that is they come and go, and are objects, i.e. 'things' that are perceived.

Awareness is the constant subject, the 'perceiver' of thoughts and sensations and that which is always present. Even during sleep there is awareness of dreams and of the quality of that sleep; and there is also awareness of sensations; if a sensation becomes strong enough, such as a sound or uncomfortable sensation, one will wake up.

All thoughts and sensations appear in awareness, exist in awareness, and subside back into awareness. Before any particular thought or sensation there is effortless awareness of 'what is': the sum of all thoughts and sensations occurring at any given instant. During the thought or sensation in question there is effortless awareness of it within 'what is'. Then when it has gone there is still effortless awareness of 'what is'.

So the body/mind is experienced as a flow of ephemeral objects appearing in this awareness, the ever present subject. For each of us any external object or thing is experienced as a combination of thought and sensation, i.e. you may see it, touch it, know what it is called, and so on. The point is that for us to be aware of anything, real or imaginary, requires thought about and/or sensation of that thing and it is awareness of these thoughts and sensations that constitutes our experience.

Therefore this awareness is the constant substratum in which all things appear to arise, exist and subside. In addition, all living things rely on awareness of their environment to exist and their behaviour is directly affected by this. At the level of living cells and above this is self-evident, but it has been shown that even electrons change their behaviour when (aware of) being observed! Thus this awareness exists at a deeper level than body/mind (and matter/energy[3]) and *we are this awareness*![4]

Awareness can also be defined as universal consciousness when it is totally at rest, completely still; aware of everything that is occurring within it. Every 'thing' that is occurring in

---

[3] The theory of relativity, and string theory, show that matter and energy are synonymous.
[4] C. Drake, *Beyond The Separate Self,* 2009, Halifax, p.18-20.

consciousness is a manifestation of cosmic energy, for the string theory[5] and the earlier theory of relativity show that matter is in fact energy, which is consciousness in motion (or motion in consciousness). For energy is synonymous with motion and consciousness is the substratum, or deepest level, of all existence.

Now all motion arises in stillness, exists in stillness, is known by its comparison with stillness, and eventually subsides back into stillness. For example, if you walk across a room, before you start there is stillness, as you walk the room is still and you know you are moving relative to this stillness, and when you stop once again there is stillness. In the same way every 'thing' (consciousness in motion, or motion in consciousness) arises in awareness (consciousness at rest), exists in awareness, is known in awareness and subsides back into awareness. Awareness is still, but is the container of all potential energy which is continually bubbling up into manifestation (physical energy) and then subsiding back into stillness. [6]

If we investigate awareness itself we can see that it is:

---

[5] This posits that all 'things' are composed of 'strings' of energy in complex configurations, vibrating at various frequencies.
[6] C. Drake, *Beyond The Separate Self,* 2009, Halifax, p.43.

Each Moment Reveals the Absolute

Effortlessly and choicelessly present, and effortlessly and choicelessly aware of all thoughts and sensations occurring in it.

Absolutely still, aware of the slightest movement of body or mind. In fact awareness is consciousness when it is completely at rest, aware of all movements that are occurring within it.

Totally silent, aware of the slightest sound or thought occurring within it.

Utterly at peace, for to be absolutely still and totally silent is to be utterly at peace.

Omnipresent, for all things (manifestations of cosmic energy) are forms of consciousness in movement, and thus arise in awareness, as all movement arises in stillness.

Omniscient, for all things exist in it, and are 'known' by it, just as all movement exists in a substratum of stillness and is known by (comparison to) that stillness.

Omnipotent, for all things subside back into it, just as all movement subsides back into stillness; and no thing has power over it.

Thus awareness is truly the source from which (and in which) all things arise, that in which all things exist and are known, and that into which all things subside. This is also:

Pure, for no thing can taint or affect it in any way.

Pristine, for no thing can degrade it.

Radiant, for it illuminates everything that appears in it.

Limitless, for it contains and encompasses all things.[7]

---

[7] C. Drake, *Beyond The Separate Self,* 2009, Halifax, p.49-51

Each Moment Reveals the Absolute

Thus awareness can be seen to include all of the properties of the Absolute posited by Eastern and Western religions, with the exception of the personal aspect of the Godhead. However, as *This* (pure awareness) is what we all are at the deeper level than body/mind, and we all have different minds and personalities, we therefore express and manifest *This* in different ways. Also as our mind/bodies are never separate from *This* but arise in *This*, exist in *This* and subside back into *This*, then *This* does indeed contain personal aspects. It's just that these are ephemeral and therefore not properties of *This*.[8]

Therefore when we investigate each moment, which is just an experience, this reveals the Absolute Reality.

---

[8] C. Drake, *Beyond The Separate Self,* 2009, Halifax, p.142

Chapter Two

A Light Unto Yourself

This chapter highlights the importance of investigating one's direct experience from the view-point of 'knowing nothing', and making one's own discoveries so that one can become 'a light unto oneself'.

'By observing mental states you also become aware of the seven factors of enlightenment. These are: awareness of awareness, investigation of the Way, vigour, joy, serenity, concentration and equanimity.' (The Buddha, Maha Sattipatthana Sutta 14-16)

The first two are paramount and the last five are outcomes of these. This is what this book and *Beyond the Separate Self* are all about, becoming 'aware of awareness' through direct investigation and then continuing with further 'investigation of the Way' (the Tao, the nature of reality). Once one is 'aware of awareness' then one can undertake further investigations not needing to relying on any 'teachings', although these may be useful for confirming what one has discovered.

I recently received the following query, from someone who had bought the book, a week after it had been purchased:

I have been reading your book with great interest but from my Course in Miracles study I understand that the ultimate being, YOU, is love. It tells us that "God is but love and therefore so are you". In the introduction we are told that we cannot learn what LOVE is but we can be taught to remove the blocks to the "awareness" of Love's Presence. "This is the Jesus teaching. I may be making a play on words here but it is probably only a different approach to the same ultimate Oneness which we all are.

Being hungry, and tired, at the time I dashed off:

Love is 'no separation' and in consciousness, at rest as pure awareness, and in motion as the manifest universe there is no separation. This consciousness in all modes is God, Allah, Brahman, The Void, The Tao ... call it what you will, Love, Colin

During lunch I realized that my reply was somewhat unhelpful so after a short rest I wrote the following:

I apologise for my somewhat brief, and unhelpful reply (although true), but I was tired and hungry. Now that I am replete and refreshed I will attempt to be more helpful.

To say that 'all is consciousness' or that 'God is Love', both of which are true, is useless unless one has realized, and experienced, the truth of these statements. That is they mean nothing until self-realization, or God-realization, has taken place.

My book is not about teachings but hopes to provide a framework in which one can investigate directly the nature of Reality, through considering one's moment-to-moment experience. To this end it seems to me that you have not approached the content in the way in which it was intended. To accomplish this one needs to take note of the following directions, which appear in Chapter one:

1: This is not a question of belief or imagination but of discovery by direct investigation, and for this to be effective we need to put aside all belief systems and acquired knowledge concerning who we are at the underlying level beyond thoughts and sensations. The only knowledge of this that is valid is that which is revealed to each one of us by direct experience. The easiest way for this direct experience to occur is by enquiring into the nature of experience itself, and for this enquiry to be effective we need to start from the position of believing and knowing nothing.

2:The chapters that follow are aids to this enquiry, and as such should not just be read and intellectually considered but need to be taken slowly, step by step, not moving onto the next step until one fully 'sees' the step that is being considered. This does not mean to say that one needs to agree with each statement, as any investigation is personal, but one needs to understand what is being said. They map the author's own investigations, over a twelve-year period, and are given in the order in which they occurred. They each stem directly from a prolonged period of meditation and contemplation, and chart a growing understanding, through experiencing and seeing, of the nature of reality and our place within it. As such they need to be taken in the order given, as each one builds on what has been 'seen' in the preceding chapters. Also to get the most out of each chapter one needs to spend some time contemplating it until one 'feels' what it is pointing to; if a chapter is just read without due attention then its significance may well be missed.[9]

By your comments about the 'Course in Miracles' it seems that you have ignored the first, and the fact that you have 'read' the book so quickly means that you have not followed the second.

Direct investigation can reveal that 'all is consciousness':

Thus there is no dichotomy or duality between the physical world and 'awareness' for they are both manifestations of the same essence. The physical universe is just cosmic energy

---

[9] C. Drake, *Beyond The Separate Self,* 2009, Halifax, p.13

(consciousness in motion) when it is manifest into physical form, and awareness (consciousness at rest) contains this same energy in latent form as potential energy.[10]

And that 'God is Love':

The word God means consciousness having two states: at rest (pure awareness), and in motion (manifestation). In this there is truly no separation as the essence and ground of all that exists is consciousness, and true love is only present where there is no separation; true love is 'no separation'. The Christian idea that 'God is Love' points to this, and love of one's fellow man naturally follows from the realization of no separation.[11]

However, for these statements to mean anything you need to have undertaken the investigation yourself and come to these realizations. In the final analysis we all have to be a 'light unto ourselves' as the Buddha says, and others can only provide pointers along the way, Love, Colin

---

[10] *Ibid* p. 43-44.
[11] *Ibid* p.95

We have all been 'taught' so much, and received so many 'teachings' but in this field of self-inquiry (or direct investigation into the nature of reality) they are useless. In fact they only act as blockages colouring our attempts at inquiry, or investigation, rendering these attempts impotent. We all need to follow Descartes in 'believing nothing' and 'doubting everything' that we have learned, taking this as the starting point for our inquiry, or investigation. It may well be that our investigations discover that which we had previously been taught, but then we will know it by our direct experience requiring no outside authority. In this case no faith or belief is necessary and any doubts can always be dispelled by our own direct investigation. What's more this investigation continually leads to further discoveries, as what is being investigated is boundless; which means that one can go beyond any external teachings and truly discover the satguru within. Then such quotes as the one that started this article are enjoyed as confirmation of what has been directly discovered, rather than needing to be 'believed' as a teaching.

Chapter Three

Separation is Suffering

This chapter considers how identifying oneself as a separate object in a universe of separate objects leads to suffering.

Separation is Suffering

Separation, that is viewing oneself as a separate being (object) in a universe of separate beings (objects) leads inexorably to suffering. Not mental and physical pain for these are part of the human condition, and thus unavoidable, but unnecessary mental suffering. Which is thinking and worrying about one's self-image, health, wealth, status, achievements, lack of achievements, past, future and ultimate survival. These are all caused by identifying oneself as an individual object in a universe of multiple objects, and also by comparing oneself with like objects (other people). How we identify ourselves is at the heart of how we view the world and our place in it. If we fail to correctly identify 'what we are' (in essence) then this leads to an unfulfilled life, with its consequent frustrations and mental suffering.

When we identify ourselves as 'separate beings' we tend to expand our concept of self-identity to include an imaginary self-image consisting of our physical appearance, mental ability, status, occupation, position in society, family situation, achievements, lack of achievements, ambitions, hopes, fears, memories and projections into the future. This naturally leads to feelings of separation and isolation; separation from our fellow man and the world we live in. Which further engenders feelings of insecurity, and fear. We tend to combat these by trying to improve this imaginary self-image, by attempting to 'better ourselves', achieve more – knowledge, possessions, power, fame, etc. – polish this self-image and generally build ourselves up. This tends to make us live in the future and stops us living fully in the present moment. The other side of this coin is to live in regret as to what might have been, self-loathing, melancholy or nostalgia and yearning for the past. This, once again, stops us seeing 'what is' here and now, either by making us live in the past or by the mind spinning on our failures and lack of self-worth.

This 'self-image' is purely a mental construct that causes much of our psychological suffering. For with no self-image, but just 'being' moment to moment, there is no fear of losing face, of not achieving or of failure, as there is nothing to protect. So separation, which implies an imaginary mind-created self-image, leads to insecurity, grasping, fear, self-cherishing and counter-productive worrying. All of this can be overcome by realizing the deeper level of being than thought/sensation (mind/body), in which there is no separation.

Chapter Four

Awakening

This chapter considers awakening and considers the function of a human being as delineated in *The Upanishads*.

Awakening

Awakening is simply a matter of rousing ourselves from the dream that we are separate objects (mind/bodies) in a universe of separate objects. This is achieved by inquiring into our own nature and discovering the deeper level in which thoughts and sensations occur, are seen, and dissolve. This rising, existing and subsiding of thoughts and sensations is an ongoing process and that which constitutes our moment-to-moment experience.

The body is experienced as a stream of sensations whilst the mind is experienced as a stream of thoughts (which includes mental images), which leaves the question of who, or what, is the experiencer? We tend to think of this as the mind but this is obviously not the deepest level of experiencing, as the mind itself (the flow of thoughts) is just an experience! Similarly with the body where sensations occur and are detected by the nervous system, and other sense organs, this too is just an experience …

So what is it that 'sees' and 'feels' these experiences, this deeper level of our being, the true experiencer and enjoyer of our existence? That which we feel we have always 'been' and that which seems to have been the constant unchanging basis of our lives.

Awakening

This is evidently not the body, for we speak of its parts as 'mine', my hand, my head, my stomach and so on … Therefore who is the owner of this complex organism? Similarly with the mind we speak of 'my thoughts on the matter are …' or 'my preference is' etc… So who is it that owns these thoughts or preferences? The problem here is that we tend to identify with the mind and these become 'I think' or 'I prefer', but this still leaves the question who is this 'I' that thinks or prefers?

The clue is that we could not survive without being aware of our thoughts and sensations (mind/body), which leads to the undeniable conclusion that it is this very awareness that is the deeper level of being … in fact who (or what) we are! For this is that in which our thoughts and sensations arise, exist, are seen, and subside. This is ever-present for whenever a thought/sensation arises there is awareness of it, and this is the witness of all our experiences, the unchanging basis of our existence.

At this point just take a few moments to notice how thoughts/sensations come and go whilst awareness, that which sees these fleeting objects, is a constant presence.

Awakening

This is pointed to by Advaita Vedanta which regards man as a physical organism through which Brahman (awareness, consciousness) senses and experiences the world. The Kena Upanishad states that it is the Self (Brahman, awareness) which is the agent and witness, through which the mind thinks and the senses experience sensations. However, this Self is undetectable by the mind and senses, being the substratum in which they appear, exist and disappear. (Kena Upanishad 1v.1-9) Moreover, due to its undetectable nature, it is very easy for man to overlook his true nature and identify with the mind and body.

The Katha Upanishad likens man to a chariot, of which the atman (the Self, awareness, Brahman within each individual) is the master, the body is the chariot, the mind is the charioteer, the sense organs are the horses and the roads they travel on are the objects of sensation. The atman is the enjoyer and experiencer of the ride, which is made possible by the charioteer, chariot and horses. (Katha Upanishad 3v.3-4) So Brahman needs the mind and senses, to enjoy and experience the physical world. However, when the mind is unaware of the master's presence, through lack of discrimination, it is unable to control the senses which run amok like wild horses (Ibid 3v.5). Brahman, pure consciousness, is hidden in every heart, being the eternal witness

Awakening

watching everything one does. He is said to be 'the operator' whilst we are his 'innumerable instruments'. (Svetasvetara Upanishad 6v.10-12) [12]

Although this is interesting it is of no use until one has become 'aware of awareness' for oneself through direct investigation of one's own moment-to-moment experience, after which the above acts as an inspiring form of confirmation of that which one has discovered.

---

[12] C. Drake, *Humanity Our Place in the Universe*, 2010, Halifax, p.55.

Chapter Five

The Myth of Doing Nothing

This chapter addresses the idea that there is nothing we can do and that everything' just happens by itself'

The Myth of Doing Nothing

I recently was talking to a friend who was complaining of existential anxiety which was dispelled by reading a good book on nonduality or attending an inspiring satsang, but which always returned. So I asked him what he 'did' on a daily basis to establish himself in nondual awareness, whereupon he grinned sheepishly indicating that he did nothing. Which made me ponder the teachings of many modern teachers of nondualism who say there is nothing to 'do' and everything just 'happens by itself'. Indeed even in my book *Beyond the Separate Self* there is a chapter entitled 'Nothing to Achieve, Find or Get' which could give the impression that there is nothing that one needs to do ... However, I can assure you that if one continues to live in the same headspace without 'doing anything' then there will no change in one's outlook and anxiety levels. For as I say in the book:

> At a deeper level than this flow of fleeting objects (thoughts and sensations) we are this constant subject, awareness itself; this is already the case and as such cannot be achieved. All that is required is to realize this!

> So awareness is central to our being, whilst thoughts and sensations are peripheral. This is self-evident for without

awareness our thoughts and sensations would pass unnoticed. Thus we cannot lose this awareness; we just need to stop overlooking it.

It is impossible to get that awareness which you already are, and thus have in full abundance. All that is required is to recognize this. In this respect you do need to 'get' this, but this is in fact nothing as it is not a thing but the 'ground' from which all things arise, in which they exist and back into which they subside. So there is in fact 'no thing to get' and you do need to 'get' nothing (ness)! [13]

So although there is:

> 'nothing to achieve,' we do need to realize the deeper level of pure awareness, for this to be the case.
>
> 'nothing to find', we do need to stop overlooking the awareness that is always present.
>
> 'nothing to get', we do need to recognize that we already have this awareness.

---

[13] C. Drake, *Beyond The Separate Self,* 2009, Halifax, p.47-49.

The Myth of Doing Nothing

This realization, or recognition, of the deeper level of pure awareness is easily accomplished by directly investigating our own moment-to-moment experience. This book and *Beyond the Separate Self* aim to provide a simple straightforward framework in which this investigation can take place. However, even after the recognition of this deeper level we do need to cultivate, and establish, this by further investigation/contemplation for as it says in *The Tibetan Book of the Dead:*

> All those of all [differing] potential, regardless of their acumen or dullness,
>
> May realize [this intrinsic awareness].
>
> However, for example, even though sesame is the source of oil and milk of butter,
>
> But there will be no extract if these are unpressed or unchurned,
>
> Similarly, even though all beings actually possess the seed of buddhahood,

> Sentient beings will not attain buddhahood without experiential cultivation.
>
> Nonetheless, even a cowherd will attain liberation if he engages in experiential cultivation.
>
> For, even though one may not know how to elucidate [this state] intellectually,
>
> One will [through experiential cultivation] become manifestly established in it.
>
> One whose mouth has actually tasted molasses,
> Does not need others to explain its taste.[14]

Even after one has 'tasted molasses' this taste will dissipate after a time, requiring further ingesting for the taste to reappear. In the same way the effect of 'awakening' to the reality of the deeper level of pure awareness will dissipate if one 'nods off' again and re-identifies with the mind/body. So one needs to continually

---

[14] Padmassambhava, *The Tibetan Book of the Dead*, transl. by Gyurme Dorje, 2006, London, p.56.

inquire into/investigate/contemplate the nature of Self and Reality for this 'awakening' to become established. It is only in this established awakening that all existential anxiety is banished.

Chapter Six

Restless Mind ... No Problem!

This chapter attempts to show that although the restless mind hinders meditation, it is no problem when relaxing into pure awareness.

Restless Mind ... No Problem!

Many people complain of a 'restless mind' when they sit down to meditate, contemplate or just relax into pure awareness. Their thoughts almost seem to speed up and a host of worldly worries crowd in that seem to make meditation, contemplation, or relaxation appear impossible. If one attempts to suppress these thoughts, or replace them with other thoughts, this often exacerbates the problem turning the river into a veritable torrent!

Now this may be a problem if one is attempting one-pointed concentration on a mantra, the breath or a symbol as in meditation. It may also seem to make contemplation, or investigation, impossible as it disturbs the flow of thoughts, dedicated to one subject, that this requires.

However, for just relaxing into pure awareness the torrent of thoughts of the 'monkey mind' or 'worry wart' is no problem at all; for in this relaxation there truly is nothing to find, achieve or acquire as awareness is already (and always) present. All that is required is to recognize this fact, which 'isn't exactly rocket science' as one would not even know that there was a 'problem' without being aware of it, which proves that awareness is already present.

Restless Mind ... No Problem!

One just needs to see (recognize) that there is awareness of this stream of thoughts/worries. This 'seeing' (recognition) has the potential to break the habit of the mind to follow these thoughts, and then they just come and go in awareness, leaving it unaffected in the same way that clouds scud across the sky, or waves appear in the ocean. Once this occurs one can then revert to contemplation or investigation if one wishes, or just remain relaxing into awareness itself.

Even if this does not occur, and the restless mind continues with its incessant chatter, this is no problem for awareness itself which just witnesses this, whilst remaining totally unconcerned. The seeing of this in turn leads to the mind letting go of all its expectations of what is required for the relaxation to deepen (i.e. that the mind should become quiet), resulting in this deepening naturally occurring. Paradoxically this can then result in the flow of discursive thoughts lessening, leading to even deeper relaxation ... But if this does not happen it's no problem!

This is where the technique of recognizing the presence of awareness, and relaxing into that, differs from other techniques that require concentration. For this seeing (recognition) has the power to diffuse thoughts (and sensations) as their ephemeral nature becomes apparent, thus making the mind less likely to scamper after them. The mind is a far more amenable servant when it can truly understand what is required of it and can see the point of this. The recognition of pure awareness leads to perfect peace, for awareness itself is always absolutely still and totally silent (being the witness to movement and thoughts/sounds) … and this is perfect peace.

Whereas, meditation on an object which requires one-pointed concentration is a somewhat artificial activity, with which the mind struggles as it fails to truly 'see' the point. It is true that if this is perfected it can lead to the same state of perfect peace, but this is not the beginner's experience. Because the mind finds it difficult to truly engage with this practice, this lack of engagement leaves the mind as restless as it was before the activity was embarked upon. In fact any attempt to artificially yoke the mind to an activity which it is unused to, and does not enjoy, often leads to the restlessness becoming more intense.

Therefore this style of meditation can become counter-productive leading to frustration and a feeling of failure. Which is a great shame for the peace of pure awareness is always present behind this intense activity and this can be readily recognized with the relevant shifting of attention. The attempt to stifle the mind to reveal this peace is often a long and arduous process which many 'meditators' fail to achieve. Even those that do 'succeed' often fail to see that this peace is ever-present and think that it can only be achieved by prolonged 'sitting'. In which case this does not lead to true freedom as this peace is not recognized as being present when one is not 'meditating'.

The other problem with 'sitting' meditation is that, for most westerners, it is not a truly comfortable occupation unaccustomed as we are to sitting cross-legged. It is true that most traditions allow beginners to sit in a chair but the implication tends to be that this is a concession and that to do the thing properly we need to learn to sit, with a straight spine, on the floor. This discomfort makes concentration even more difficult to achieve, as if the activity was not tricky enough already! Whereas relaxing into pure awareness can be done in any position and is best done where there is no discomfort whatsoever.

In my case I spent over 20 years involved in this style of meditation performed in twice daily sittings of 30-60 minutes. Whilst this lead to many beautiful experiences, trance states (and sore knees!) it never lead to total freedom. For it always left me feeling that there was more to achieve which would occur through even greater effort. It was only when I was told to 'STOP', give up all effort, and simply ask 'Who am I?' that the penny dropped and I realized that I, as a separate entity, do not exist (Anatta)! All that was there was the ever-present awareness of the thoughts/sensations.

Some amazing experiences also followed but this discovery that 'I' do not exist is the key and is repeated every time I look to see 'Who am I?' Further than this is the recognition of pure awareness itself in which thoughts/sensations arise, exist, are seen and subside. This has left me completely free from all existential angst, with a feeling of being totally 'at home in the universe' and experiencing a simple 'ease of being'. None of this was true during all my years of rigorous rigid mantra/breath/visualization meditations. I now know that in fact there is nothing to achieve, find or get, for awareness is always present. All that is required is just 'being' moment to moment identified as this awareness of thoughts and sensations. Then if deeper experiences come, beautiful, and if not… no problem. Truly each moment is enough!

It is interesting to note that, after what I have said about mantra, I sometimes use mantra to aid me relaxing into this pure awareness; which I do for the joy of it, rather than to achieve, find, or get anything. The mantra I use is 'Om Namah Sivaya' which means 'salutations to pure awareness (or consciousness) which is the Absolute Totality of Being'. As this is repeated it points directly to this pure awareness by its meaning and the experiential fact of awareness of the repetition. About this Nisargadatta said:

> Recite the sacred name, that is all right, but the important thing is to recognize and understand what is the presiding principle [awareness] by which you know you are and by which you perceive everything else.[15]

It is this attention on the awareness itself that is the key, for this awareness is always absolutely still and totally silent, which is perfect peace. This meaning and the noticing of awareness has the power to diffuse the restless mind, especially after some practice where the value of relaxing into awareness itself has been experienced. Mantra repetition also reveals the 'nothingness' relative to which all 'things' can be recognized. For the thought

---

[15] http://nisargadatta.co.cc/pages/quotes_consciousness_and_absolute.html

is known (there is awareness of it) relative to the no-thought in which it appears.

This is the 'nothingness' which can be revealed by repeating the mantra with intense concentration, thus blocking out all other 'things' from the mind. However, this nothingness may be immediately realized by seeing that every 'thing' appears in nothingness, exists in nothingness, is known relative to this nothingness and disappears back into nothingness. Without this background of nothingness there would not be awareness of any 'thing'. As the only things in our direct experience are thoughts (including all mental images) and sensations, awareness of which is only possible due to contrast with the 'nothingness' in which they appear, then this 'nothingness' is absolutely vital for awareness of any 'thing'; and is in fact a property of awareness itself. 'Consciousness at rest' (awareness) implies the 'subjective field' which is conscious (aware) and still, that is 'nothingness' as all 'things' are forms of cosmic energy, and thus in motion.

So if one repeats the mantra (or any mantra) noticing the awareness of the repetition and the nothingness (no thought) in which it arises, exists and subsides, then the mantra has done its job in revealing the nature of reality. In fact every single thing in manifestation points directly to this 'aware nothingness', or 'formless awareness', in exactly the same way. For it is in contrast to the nothingness that any thing is perceived, and awareness is that which underlies perception, in that one is effortlessly and choicelessly aware of sense (and mind) perceptions. However, mantra repetition has the added advantage of pointing to this directly by its form and meaning, for every mantra extols different aspects of this Absolute Reality. This 'aware nothingness', or 'formless awareness', is: Jehovah, God the Father, Allah, Brahman, Siva, The Void (Theravadan Buddhism), Rigpa (Tibetan Buddhism), Big Mind (Zen), and The Tao. Mystics of all persuasions who follow the 'negative path' have come to this same realization of the Absolute Reality, although they give it different names.

Chapter Seven

Memories are Made of This

This chapter considers how memories give the illusion of a 'separate self' and shows how investigation can debunk this.

Memories are Made of This

I recently received the following query, which I think many of us can relate to, from a reader of *Beyond the Separate Self:*

Hi Colin,

I have been reading Dialogue in Consciousness and I was wondering if you could answer a question I have about something I read. It said that memory is just a concept. So does that mean that when teachers say nothing exists that they literally mean nothing exists? What came up for me when I read that memory is a concept was that literally nothing existed before this moment – not even a minute ago – and that there is no past. Does that mean that there whatever is happening is happening freshly now and that all my so-called memories don't exist at all? It feels huge but my mind doesn't want to accept this at all – if in fact this is what the writer meant about memories being concepts. But what then comes up is well why does it seem to have continuity? I go to work and I know what to do, I recognise some people and others appear to be total strangers. I can see pictures of myself as a child. How is that all explained? All that seems to come from memory. I remember how to do things, I remember people – and everything always seems to be there the next time. But sometimes I also wonder if people are still there when I'm not

Memories are Made of This

there. I hope you don't mind me asking you these questions. I just wanted to run it by someone before my mind whitewashes over it.

Here is my reply:

To say that memory is just a concept means that memories are just ephemeral thoughts (including all mental images), they come and go. Recognition occurs by comparison of these 'images', which have been stored by past sense-impressions, with the present sense-perceptions. Whereas, that which 'sees' these thoughts/images is the constant conscious subjective presence of pure awareness.

However, this does not mean that they are not useful; in fact as you have pointed out they are vital for our survival and seem to provide a sense of continuity of an apparent separate self. When examined carefully this can be seen to be an illusion as all thoughts/images (and therefore memories) come and go, whereas the continuing presence is in fact awareness itself. The confusion arises when we identify ourselves with the mind, i.e. with the thought/recognition process, rather than seeing the mind as what it is: a very powerful tool (our onboard computer) which allows us to negotiate the physical world.

This does not mean that the mind is not a part of what we are, but that it only exists at a peripheral level and is experienced as a flow of objects (thoughts and mental images). At the deeper level we are the experiencer, the constant conscious subject (pure awareness), and identifying with this means that memories lose their power to overwhelm us as we can see them for what they are, just a flow of ephemeral objects. A very useful flow at times but not who (or what) we are at the deepest level.

As far as 'nothing existing' is concerned, at the ultimate level all (every thing) is just the 'play of consciousness'. All things are manifestations of cosmic energy (movements in consciousness, or consciousness in movement) and arise in, and from, consciousness at rest (pure awareness) which is aware of the movements occurring within it. They exist in this (and are 'seen' by this) and finally subside back into this. So the phrase 'nothing exists' means that no thing is permanent, or has a primary individual irreducible essence.

I do hope that this answers your question(s), love, Colin

Memories are Made of This

An inquirer read in a book,
That memory is just a concept,
This her whole foundation shook,
"No past (self)' she could not accept.

For memory is a paradoxical thread,
On which seeming continuity revolves.
If not believed our 'story' we could shed,
And watch as our 'small self' dissolves.

However, it is a useful tool,
For living our day to day lives,
On this our knowing we spool,
Thus objects can we recognise.

Every thing that we meet,
Our mind compares with this store,
So our experience we can greet,
Informed by what's gone before.

But memories can easily create,
The illusion of a separate being,
If their meaning we overstate,
Not their impermanence seeing.

In fact they just come and go,
In the constant subjective presence,
Ephemeral objects that flow,
In Awareness, our true essence.

So, although memory has its use,
Past memories can delude,
Causing us identity to confuse,
With the story that's viewed.

Chapter Eight

Nonduality

This chapter shows how the investigation of experience can lead to the recognition of nonduality.

Nonduality

Nonduality – not 'the quality or opposition of being dual (two).'
not 'the opposition between two concepts or
aspects.' (Oxford English Dictionary)

Or to put it simply 'not two' (of anything). It is put this way, rather than saying 'all is one', for the very term 'one' implies (that there could be) two or more… In fact the term 'nonmultiplicity' would be more accurate for what is being suggested here is 'not many' rather than 'not two'.

What we are trying to get a handle on here is that there is actually no (permanently existing) thing in existence and that all apparent 'things' are manifestations of the same essence.

This can be shown by investigating the nature of our own subjective experiences, which is actually all that any of us have to investigate. For each of us any external object or thing is experienced as a combination of thought (including mental images) and sensation, i.e. you may see it, touch it, know what it is called, and so on … Thus everything in the external world is experienced as a mixture of thoughts and sensations, and when we attempt to investigate any 'thing' it is these that we are investigating.

In any given moment of direct experience there are only three elements: thoughts (including all mental images), sensations (everything detected by the senses) and awareness of these thoughts and sensations. All thoughts and sensations are ephemeral objects (the perceived) which appear in this awareness (the perceiver) which is the constant subject. So at a deeper level than the ever-changing objects (thoughts and sensations) we are this constant subject, awareness itself.

To put this in a slightly different way, we can easily notice that every thought and sensation occurs in awareness, exists in awareness and dissolves back into awareness. Before any particular thought or sensation there is effortless awareness of 'what is': the sum of all thoughts and sensations occurring at any given instant. During the thought or sensation in question there is effortless awareness of it within 'what is'. Then when it has gone there is still effortless awareness of 'what is'.

Reiterating, for each of us any external object (or thing) is experienced as a combination of thought and sensation, i.e. you see it, touch (feel) it, know what it is called, etc. Therefore in our direct experience everything arises in, exists in and subsides back into awareness itself.

Awareness can also be defined as universal consciousness when it is totally at rest, completely still; aware of every movement that is occurring within it. In our direct experience we can see that awareness is still, as there is awareness of the slightest movement of mind or body. In fact this is the 'stillness' relative to which any movement can be known. Every 'thing' that is occurring in consciousness is a manifestation of cosmic energy, for the string theory[16] and the earlier theory of relativity show that matter is in fact energy, which is consciousness in motion (or motion in consciousness). For energy is synonymous with motion and consciousness is the substratum, or deepest level, of all existence.

Now all motion arises in stillness, exists in stillness, is known by its comparison with stillness, and eventually subsides back into stillness. For example, if you walk across a room, before you start there is stillness, as you walk the room is still and you know you are moving relative to this stillness, and when you stop once

---

[16] This posits that all 'things' are composed of 'strings' of energy in complex configurations, vibrating at various frequencies.

again there is stillness. In the same way every 'thing' (consciousness in motion) arises in awareness (consciousness at rest), exists in awareness, is known in awareness and subsides back into awareness. Awareness is still, but is the container of all potential energy which is continually bubbling up into manifestation (physical energy) and then subsiding back into stillness.

Thus there is no dichotomy or duality between the physical world and 'awareness' for they are both manifestations of the same essence. The physical universe is just cosmic energy (consciousness in motion) when it is manifest into physical form, and awareness (consciousness at rest) contains this same energy in latent form as potential energy. Therefore there is in reality no multiplicity (nonduality) as there is only consciousness existing in two modes, in motion and at rest.[17]

---

[17] C. Drake, *Beyond The Separate Self,* 2009, Halifax, p.41-44.

Chapter Nine

Awakening is Not an Experience

This chapter highlights the fact that awakening is a recognition, or realization, rather than an experience.

Awakening is Not an Experience

I recently received a query from a long-time Christian reader of my book who said that he is yearning for the experience of awakening. Here is my reply, note that all of the quotes (the indented passages) are from *Beyond the Separate Self*:

It should be noted that awakening is not an experience but a realization (or recognition) of a deeper level of being than mind/body. As I say in the book:

> The problem is that enlightenment, freedom, *moksha*, liberation, *nirvana*, call it what you will, has been described in such glowing terms that we expect it to be an ecstatic, unforgettable experience. Whereas the realization, that at a deeper level than mind/body one is awareness itself, may seem so obvious as to be 'nothing special'. The consequences of this realization may lead to ecstatic experiences, but these should not be confused with the realization itself. However, if this realization is 'cultivated' so that one becomes completely identified with awareness itself, then this is enlightenment, freedom, *moksha*, liberation, *nirvana*.[18]

---

[18] C. Drake, *Beyond The Separate Self,* 2009, Halifax, p.61.

Awakening is Not an Experience

This realization is achieved by direct investigation of one's moment-to-moment experience (see chapter two[19]) which reveals this 'deeper level'. Before this investigation is attempted one needs to take note of this advice from chapter one:

> This is not a question of belief or imagination but of discovery by direct investigation, and for this to be effective we need to put aside all belief systems and acquired knowledge concerning who we are at the underlying level beyond thoughts and sensations. The only knowledge of this that is valid is that which is revealed to each one of us by direct experience. The easiest way for this direct experience to occur is by enquiring into the nature of experience itself, and for this enquiry to be effective we need to start from the position of believing and knowing nothing.

However, I realize this negation of previous acquired learning may be difficult for you to achieve, so if you find this impossible let me try to put this into a more Christian context. You just need to slightly redefine your terms in such a way that previous <u>concepts will not act as a barr</u>ier to your investigation:

[19] Chapter one in this book.

God – The Absolute, or Ultimate, Reality which underlies the whole of creation.

Soul – The deeper level of being than thoughts/sensations (mind/body).

Heaven – Identifying with this deeper level of being, which leads to (comm) union with the Absolute.

Hell – Identifying with mind/body, negation of this Absolute.

Awakening – The realization of 'the kingdom of heaven within you' (identification with this deeper level) followed by the cultivation of (and committing to) this realization.

I would recommend that you carry out this investigation at least three times daily, using chapter two[20], as your 'template' until the realization becomes established. As you do this take note of the prequel:

> Each step should be considered until one experiences, or 'sees', its validity before moving on to the following step. If you reach a step where you do not find this possible, continue on regardless in the same way, and hopefully the flow of the investigation will make this step clear. By all

---

[20] Chapter one in this book.

means examine each step critically but with an open mind, for if you only look for 'holes' that's all you will find![21]

Once you fully 'see' what is being said by your own direct investigation of your moment-to-moment experience then you can move on to the later chapters. This direct 'seeing' may lead to ecstatic 'experiences', but also may not:

> These experiences vary greatly from person to person and are ultimately irrelevant as the recognition and realization of one's own essential nature is the crucial factor for attaining freedom. [22]

I hope this is of some help, Love, Colin

P.S. Even after my first 'awakening' I have followed the process I outlined to you. I have found (and so there's nor reason to assume you won't too) that it leads to further 'discoveries', life becoming 'lighter' and less 'heavy', and an undercurrent of joy and peace. In the long run this is more valuable than any ephemeral experience.

> Experiences come and go,
> In That by which our minds can know,

---

[21] C. Drake, *Beyond The Separate Self*, 2009, Halifax, p.18.
[22] *Ibid* p.24.

Awakening is Not an Experience

Thoughts and images when they show,
And sensations as they to and fro.

The Knower which is ever behind
The ephemeral body/mind.
A constant conscious subjective presence,
Our fundamental innermost essence.

For each of us the world is made,
Of experiences which appear and fade,
In Awareness which is ever here,
Closer than close, nearer than near.

If to yourself you wish to be kind,
Avoid identifying with the mind.
Just a flow of images and thought,
In That which need never be sought.

To awaken identify with the latter,
The source, ground and end of all matter.
See that you are the permanent
Awareness, and thus ever content.

This awakening is not an experience,
Nor with thoughts and images a dalliance.
A realization of That which never changes,
In which cosmic energy just re-arranges.

Many experiences may it evoke,
They varied greatly in those who awoke.
But freedom is seeing 'I am That',
And the cultivation of this fact!

Chapter Ten

Awareness a No-Brainer!

This article was written in reply to the assertion that awareness cannot exist without a brain.

Awareness a No-Brainer!

In reply to a recent article of mine a critic wrote: 'There cannot be any awareness unless there is one who is aware and, what/who is it that is aware? The brain of course! Before the brain existed & upon its death there was no & will be no awareness.'

This is the mind's central argument against the realization that deeper than mind/body (which is experienced as a flow of thoughts/mental images/physical sensations) is pure awareness. (Further than that, this is what we are at this deepest level!) The argument goes that without the brain 'we' would not be aware (of anything); therefore upon its death there will be no awareness. This argument is based on a misunderstanding of the word 'awareness', which is quite understandable as I use this word in a very particular way. Which I hope will be made clear by the following excerpt from *Beyond the Separate Self*:

> Before starting we need to discuss the nature of awareness itself. It is obvious that we would not 'know' (be aware of) our own perceptions without awareness being present. This does not mean that we are always conscious of each one of them, as this is dictated by where we put our attention, or upon what we focus our mind. However, all sensations detected by the body, and thoughts/mental

images occurring in the mind, appear in awareness, and we can readily become conscious of them by turning our attention to them. So awareness is like the screen on which all of our thoughts and sensations appear, and the mind becomes conscious of these by focusing on them. Take, for example, what happens when you open your eyes and look at a beautiful view: everything seen immediately appears in awareness, but for the mind to make anything of this it needs to focus upon certain elements of what is seen. 'There is an amazing tree', 'wow look at that eagle', 'what a stunning sky', etc. To be sure, you may just make a statement like 'what a beautiful view', but this does not in itself say much and is so self-evident as to be not worth saying!

The point is that the mind is a tool for problem-solving, information storing, retrieval and processing, and evaluating the data provided by our senses. It achieves this by focusing on specific sensations, thoughts or mental images that are present in awareness, and 'processing' these. In fact we only truly see 'things as they are' when they are not seen through the filter of the mind, and this occurs when what is encountered is able to 'stop the mind'. For instance we have all had glimpses of this at various times in our lives, often when seeing a beautiful sunset, a waterfall or some other wonderful natural phenomenon. These may seem other-worldly or intensely vivid, until the mind kicks in with any evaluation when everything seems to return to 'normal'. In fact nature is much more vivid and alive when directly perceived, and the more we identify with the 'perceiver', as awareness itself, the more frequently we see things 'as they are'. [23]

So I differentiate between becoming 'conscious' of something which means the mind 'seeing' it, which requires a brain, and awareness itself which is the substratum in which these 'things' occur. So when there is no mind (brain) there is indeed no 'consciousness' of thoughts, mental images or sensations.

In fact one of the great values of having a sophisticated mind is that it can become 'aware of awareness'. So a human birth is indeed fortunate for it gives us the opportunity to achieve what the Buddha calls: 'the first factor of enlightenment', which is 'awareness of awareness'. This is easy to see by sitting quietly

---

[23] C. Drake, *Beyond The Separate Self,* 2009, Halifax, p.14-15.

and noticing how thoughts and sensations come and go, whilst 'awareness' is a constant conscious subjective presence.

However, even if you reject this concept of awareness, at the level of 'becoming conscious of something' it is easy to demonstrate that this does not necessarily require a brain; for all living things rely on awareness of their environment to exist and their behaviour is directly affected by this. This does show some ability to process incoming data and act (or react) according to this, but does not imply a 'brain' in the normal definition of the word [24] ... At the level of living cells and above this is self-evident, but it has been shown that even electrons change their behaviour when (aware of) being observed! Thus this awareness exists at a deeper level than body/mind (and matter/energy[25]) and at the deepest level *we are this awareness*! About this Sogyal Rinpoche says, 'In Tibetan we call it Rigpa, a primordial, pure, pristine awareness that is at once intelligent, cognizant, radiant and always awake …. It is in fact the nature of everything'[26].

---

[24] 'Organ of soft nervous tissue contained in the skull', or 'intellectual capacity' (OED)
See also 'What brainless moulds may teach us' Deborah Smith, Sydney Morning Herald, September 4, 2010
[25] The theory of relativity, and string theory, show that matter and energy are synonymous.
[26] S. Rinpoche *The Tibetan Book of Living and Dying*, 1992, San Francisco p.47

Awareness a No-Brainer!

A materialist critic quipped:
Awareness needs someone, who is aware,
Requiring that one be equipped,
With a brain, or else it cannot be there!

This is the central argument of the mind,
Our investigations to bedevil,
Making it more difficult to find,
Neath body/mind, the deeper level.

Awareness in which these must always be,
Thoughts, images, sensations - objects that flow,
In this subjective presence by which we see,
Our experiences as they come and go.

Showing no brain is needed is child's play.
Consider electrons whose behaviour is changed
By being observed, so we could say,
They are aware of circumstances when rearranged.

Or white corpuscles in the blood,
Attacking foreign bodies that invade,
Thus nipping illness in the bud,
By awareness of threats that could degrade.

And brainless moulds that thrive and grow,
In damp and fetid situations,
When aware of food towards it they flow,
Requiring no mental cogitations!

As Descartes said – ourselves we know,
By internal awareness of thoughts and existence,
Innate in all beings, preceding the 'show',
Of reflection, knowledge and cognizance.

Chapter Eleven

The Fundamental Secret

This chapter discusses a secret which is much more fundamental than that described in the movie (and book) 'The Secret'.

The Fundamental Secret

The movie 'The Secret' proposes that one can get what one wants by applying 'the law of attraction'. 'Ask, believe and receive' is the motto of those that wish to create abundance by applying the power of their mind and positive thinking. However, there is a much more fundamental secret by which one can realize that one is, at the deepest level, totally abundant and lacking nothing ... even if it appears this is not the case at the surface level of body/mind. When this realization kicks in one finds that 'each moment is enough, or perfect, in itself' and this leaves one truly 'wanting nothing', in both senses of the phrase! Then 'asking, believing and receiving' is truly too much effort, and even the thought of 'positive thinking' seems positively exhausting!

This deeper level is always present, for it is within this that the body/mind appear, and can be readily discovered by direct investigation into one's moment to moment experience:

1. Consider the following statement: 'Life, for each of us, is just a series of moment-to-moment experiences'. These experiences start when we are born and continue until we die, rushing headlong after each other, so that they seem to merge into a whole that we call 'my life'. However, if we stop to look we can readily see that, for each of us, every moment is just an experience.

2. Any moment of experience has only three elements: thoughts (including all mental images), sensations (everything sensed by the body and its sense organs) and awareness of these thoughts and sensations. Emotions and feelings are a combination of thought and sensation.

3. Thoughts and sensations are ephemeral, that is they come and go, and are objects, i.e. 'things' that are perceived.

4. Awareness is the constant subject, the 'perceiver' of thoughts and sensations and that which is always present. Even during sleep there is awareness of dreams and of the quality of that sleep; and there is also awareness of sensations; if a sensation becomes strong enough, such as a sound or uncomfortable sensation, one will wake up.

5. All thoughts and sensations appear in awareness, exist in awareness, and subside back into awareness. Before any particular thought or sensation there is effortless awareness of 'what is': the sum of all thoughts and sensations occurring at any given instant. During the thought or sensation in question there is

effortless awareness of it within 'what is'. Then when it has gone there is still effortless awareness of 'what is'.

6. So the body/mind is experienced as a flow of ephemeral objects appearing in this awareness, the ever present subject. For each of us any external object or thing is experienced as a combination of thought and sensation, i.e. you may see it, touch it, know what it is called, and so on. The point is that for us to be aware of anything, real or imaginary, requires thought about and/or sensation of that thing and it is awareness of these thoughts and sensations that constitutes our experience.

7. Therefore this awareness is the constant substratum in which all things appear to arise, exist and subside. In addition, all living things rely on awareness of their environment to exist and their behaviour is directly affected by this. At the level of living cells and above this is self-evident, but it has been shown that even electrons change their behaviour when (aware of) being observed! Thus this awareness exists at a deeper level than body/mind (and matter/energy[27]) and *we are this awareness*!

---

[27] The theory of relativity, and string theory, show that matter and energy are synonymous.

8. This does not mean that at a surface level we are not the mind and body, for they arise in, are perceived by and subside back into awareness, which is the deepest and most fundamental level of our being. However, if we choose to identify with this deepest level – awareness – (the perceiver) rather than the surface level, mind/body (the perceived), then thoughts and sensations are seen for what they truly are, just ephemeral objects which come and go, leaving awareness itself totally unaffected.[28]

This awareness is always present, for without it we would not be aware of our own thoughts and sensations. Once we see this and can identify with this deeper level of awareness then it can be readily realized that 'each moment is enough, or perfect, in itself', as awareness just witnesses 'what is' at any given moment without wishing to achieve or change anything. Then this 'each moment is enough' becomes a powerful tool to overcome boredom, insomnia, mental restlessness, mind created suffering etc… For awareness itself is never afflicted by these problems, and identification with this gives perfect peace for awareness is always still and silent, which is perfect peace.

---

[28] C. Drake, *Beyond The Separate Self,* 2009, Halifax, p.18-20

I have found that 'each moment is enough', and identification with this deeper level, is a marvellous way to overcome boredom whilst on long flights, as the time seems to pass miraculously and boredom completely vanishes for awareness itself is never bored. In fact boredom is a property of the mind caused by it judging every moment and seeking to change 'what is' to suit its own preferences, whereas awareness itself is always content and at peace.

This 'each moment is enough' is also a great way to overcome insomnia, for once the mind identifies with awareness it stops worrying about sleeplessness. When this occurs sleep automatically takes over if the mind is tired and if not the peace provided by identifying with awareness provides refreshment and relaxation.

So for me 'each moment is enough', which implies identification with the pure awareness that one already is at the deepest level, is the fundamental secret. This leaves one 'wanting no thing' and 'being nothing' for awareness is not a thing, but is the constant conscious field of subjectivity which sees, or witnesses, everything appearing in it.

In fact 'each moment is enough' can be a 'magic bullet' to remove all mental anxiety and agitation. If these do occur then they too can be a wake up call to the fact that we have stopped identifying at the deeper level and are back at the surface level of body/mind.

This book and *Beyond the Separate Self* aim to provide a framework in which one can investigate directly the nature of Reality, through considering one's moment-to-moment experience. Once the discovery of the deeper level of pure awareness has occurred then one can replace 'ask, believe and receive' with 'investigate, realize and relax'!

Chapter Twelve

Awareness of Awareness

This chapter highlights the differences between thought and awareness and shows the importance of recognizing this.

Awareness of Awareness

'By observing mental states you also become aware of the seven factors of enlightenment. These are: **awareness of awareness**, **investigation of the Way**, vigour, joy, serenity, concentration and equanimity.' (The Buddha, Maha Sattipatthana Sutta 14-16)

The first two are paramount and the last five are outcomes of these. This is what my book *Beyond the Separate Self* is all about, becoming 'aware of awareness' through direct investigation and then continuing with further 'investigation of the Way' (the Tao, the nature of reality). Once one is 'aware of awareness' then one can undertake further investigations not needing to relying on any teachings, although these may be useful for confirming what one has discovered.

I recently received an e-mail from a reader who said they could not tell the difference between 'awareness' and thought. I replied that I did not see how this was possible (please excuse my lack of acumen) and suggested that he consider the following:

(A) Thought   (The) Awareness

A 'sound' in the mind.   That which 'hears' this sound.

Awareness of Awareness

An object, some 'thing'.	The subject of this 'thing'.
The 'thing' that is witnessed.	The witness of this 'thing'.
The (thing that is) seen.	The seer.
A movement in the mind.	The aware stillness.
The (thing that is) known	The knower (of the thing).
That which comes & goes.	That which is always here.
An object of experience.	The experiencer.

So awareness is the constant conscious subjective presence which is aware of ephemeral objects (thoughts and sensations, mind and body) as they come and go.

'Awareness of Awareness' is the key to awakening by the path of self-knowledge (Jnana), which is the most straightforward of the many paths available. Once one has become 'aware of awareness' then awakening is a direct result of this and the continuing investigation of this.

This is extremely simple, almost obvious, just the acknowledgement of the fact that one is aware of one's thoughts/mental images/sensations and that this awareness is always present whereas thoughts/mental images/sensations come and go. The danger is that the mind will dismiss this as being too simple (and obvious) and therefore of no value. I urge you not to allow this, for if you do you will be overlooking the most precious realization. The mind naturally does this as it is not in its interests to acknowledge this recognition, for this will undermine its central dominant position.

Most people identify with their minds as being what they 'are' and this becoming 'aware of awareness' has the potential to completely destroy this illusion. So the mind will try to negate this 'seeing'; the simple solution to this is, when it comes to reality, *don't believe a single thought.* Just rely on immediate direct experience, and this direct experience that you are awareness can be had instantly. As soon as the mind carries on with its doubts, questions and tricks, notice that you are effortlessly aware of every thought. If you then just watch the thoughts from pure awareness, without following a single one, they soon quieten down and give up. [29]

This is an ongoing process but it is no cause for despondency. For every time this occurs these negative thoughts can make you turn to awareness itself and in awareness there is only serenity and peace ... In fact, in the same way, every single thing in existence is a pointer towards awareness. For everything perceived appears in this pure awareness that you are.

This is easy to see by investigating the nature of one's moment-to-moment experience, and my book aims to provide a framework within which this investigation may be successfully carried out. This results in becoming 'aware of awareness', after which one can carry out deeper investigations into the nature of reality with this awareness (of awareness) as the starting point.

The great masters say that there is no end to awakening and spiritual experience, there's always more to be found – what a wonderful idea! Sri Ramakrishna used to continually tell his devotees to 'go forward' and make further discoveries. You will find this is more than an idea, for you will discover that the

---

[29] C. Drake, *Beyond The Separate Self,* 2009, Halifax, p.36-37.

deeper you go, the more you become 'aware of awareness', the more that will be revealed.

Chapter Thirteen

Hakuin's Song of Freedom

A beautiful expression of freedom, from the Mahayana School, with commentary in italics.

For such as, reflecting within themselves,
Testify to the truth of Self-nature,
To the truth that Self-nature is no-nature,

Upon enquiring 'who am I' one discovers that no separate individual exists.
Or on investigating awareness one discovers that one is this (universal) awareness.

They have really gone beyond the ken of sophistry,
For them opens the gate of oneness of cause and effect,

They have gone beyond conceptual knowledge, and discovered that cause and effect both appear in, exist in, and return to awareness, the universal subject.

And straight runs the path of non-duality and non-trinity,
Abiding with the not-particular which is in particulars,

Within this discovery there is no duality, as everything is seen to be just a movement in consciousness. That is cosmic energy, which arises in, exists in, and subsides back into awareness (consciousness at rest). This is the not-particular which is the substratum in which all 'particulars', impermanent objects, exist.

Whether going or returning, they remain for ever unmoved;
Taking hold of the no-thought which lies in thoughts,

Remaining identified as awareness, in which all thoughts come and go, they are unaffected by external circumstances.

In every act of theirs they hear the voice of truth,
How boundless the sky of Samadhi unfettered!

They live in a state of Sahaj Samadhi, natural spontaneity, in which every act comes from awareness itself.

How transparent the perfect moonlight of the Fourfold Wisdom!
At that moment what do they lack?

There is full realization of the 'four noble truths': that there is suffering; suffering is a result of craving caused by spiritual ignorance; there is a way of overcoming this craving; this is by realizing the truths of anatta, no self, and annica, impermanence. In this realization each moment is enough, or perfect, in itself.

As the Truth eternally calm reveals itself to them,
This very earth is the Lotus Land of Purity,
And this body is the body of the Buddha.

As one lives in this revelation of the Truth, that one <u>is</u> pure awareness, which is ever still and at peace, then this very existence becomes 'heaven on earth'; and this very body is known to be the instrument of awareness itself.

Chapter Fourteen

Investigation/Inquiry more: Observing than Thinking.
Noticing than Wondering.
Experiment than Opinion.

This chapter discusses the fact that investigation/inquiry has to be experiential rather than intellectual and that the realization it produces needs to be cultivated to become established.

Investigation/Inquiry Experiential not Intellectual

A critic recently said that he had realized the deeper level of awareness but that this had caused no real change in his anxiety level. This is because this realization was intellectual rather than experiential, or because this had not been cultivated by repeated investigation/inquiry.

Realization can be the outcome of investigating the nature of experience, resulting from observing, or noticing, that thoughts/mental images/sensations are ephemeral objects which come and go within awareness, which is the constant conscious subjective presence. It is easy to notice this by just taking a few moments sitting quietly and experiencing that this is the case; by watching how these thoughts/mental images/sensations come and go, appearing in awareness which is already, and always, present.

The logical outcome of this is that this unchanging presence is what we are, at the deepest level, within which our experiences of our mind/bodies (the flow of thoughts/mental images/sensations) come and go, appear and disappear, arise and subside.

This is also easy to notice, for when there is no thought/mental image there is no (experience of the) mind, and when there is no physical sensation there is no experience of the body. However, awareness is always present, ready, as it were, to 'see' any thought/mental image/sensation that may arise. This realization requires observation, or noticing, more than thinking or wondering. Although wondering is a useful first step to initiate the investigation, and thinking may be a useful tool to draw conclusions about what has been discovered.

Once this discovery has been made then one can devise experiments to investigate this awareness in an attempt to uncover its properties. For example raise a thought, such as 'Om Namah Shivaya', and then check out the awareness of this thought:

1/ Observe whether any effort is required to be aware of any thought/mental image/sensation.
This readily reveals that this awareness is effortlessly present and effortlessly aware... It requires no effort by the mind/body and they cannot make it vanish however much effort they apply.

2/ Observe whether there is any choice in becoming aware of thoughts/mental images/sensations. This also reveals that this awareness is choicelessly present and choicelessly aware. Once again it requires no choice of the body/mind and they cannot block it however, they try. i.e. If you have a toothache there is

Investigation/Inquiry Experiential not Intellectual

effortless awareness of it and the mind/body cannot choose for this not to be the case. You may think that this is bad news but that is not the case, can you imagine if you had to make a choice whether you would like to be aware for every sensation that the body experiences! In fact be grateful that there is no effort or choice involved for awareness just to be...such ease and simplicity...which is not surprising for you are this awareness!

3/ Observe whether you can ever experiences a time or place when awareness is not present. Even during sleep there is awareness of dreams, the quality of the sleep, and bodily sensations, in that if a noise is loud enough or a feeling (of pain or discomfort for instance) is strong enough it will bring the mind back to the conscious state, i.e. One will wake up... The natural conclusion to this is that for each of us awareness is omnipresent, i.e. always present. Once again be grateful that the mind/body is never required to search for this awareness, it is just always there, which of course is not surprising for one is this awareness.

4/ Next notice that this awareness is absolutely still for it is aware of the slightest movement of body or mind. For example we all know that to be completely 'aware' of what is going on around us in a busy environment we have to be completely still, just witnessing the activity.

5/ In the same vein this awareness can be 'seen' to be totally silent as it is aware of the slightest sound, the smallest thought. The natural conclusion to be drawn is that awareness is always in a state of perfect peace for complete stillness and total silence is perfect peace.

6/ Notice that awareness is omniscient, in that every thought/mental image/sensation appears in it, exists in it, is known by it, and disappears back into it. Before any particular thought or sensation there is effortless awareness of 'what is' (the sum of all thoughts and sensations occurring at any given instant), during the thought or sensation in question there is effortless awareness of it within 'what is', and then when it has gone there is still effortless awareness of 'what is'.

7/ Finally notice that every thought/mental image/sensation is 'seen' by the 'light' of awareness, i.e. awareness is radiant.[30]

---

[30] C. Drake, *Beyond The Separate Self,* 2009, Halifax, p.20-22.

Investigation/Inquiry Experiential not Intellectual

So now we have reached the 'Radiant, still, silent, omnipresent, omniscient, ocean of effortless, choiceless, awareness' (the Absolute without form or attributes) which, at the deepest level, we all are! Give up all striving, seeking and desiring, and just identify with This which you already are... Identification with This, rather than with body/mind (thought, mental images and sensations), gives instant peace for awareness is always 'still and silent' totally unaffected by whatever appears in it.

The point is that realization requires observation/experience rather than purely intellectual recognition. It's like the difference between seeing, smelling, feeling, bathing in and tasting the ocean, and reading about it in a book. Then it truly is a case of 'seeing is believing' which may lead to an opinion which will be grounded in one's own discoveries. When it comes to reality the only knowledge that is valid is that which is revealed to each one of us by direct experience and the easiest way for this direct experience to occur is by inquiring into the nature of experience itself.

Also the effect of awakening to the reality of the deeper level of pure awareness will dissipate if one 'nods off' again and re-identifies with the mind/body. So one needs to continually

Investigation/Inquiry Experiential not Intellectual

inquire into, investigate and contemplate the nature of Self and Reality until this awakening becomes established. It is only in this established awakening that all existential anxiety is banished.

Chapter Fifteen

Nonduality and Religion

This chapter considers how the religions of the world define the dual in the nondual.

Nonduality and Religion

At the Science and Nonduality Conference: The popularity of nonduality continues to grow. One of the key-note speakers confirmed or suggested such when he said we are witnessing the breaking away of spirituality from religion and that it is breaking down rapidly. However, nonduality is the core of the world's major religions, and to suggest that they are irrelevant to the popularity/pursuit of nonduality is an oversimplification. Below is a selection of nondual ideas from the world's five major religions. The first two pairs are from Vedanta, the next four from Judaism/Christianity, followed by two from Islam, three from Hinduism and finally three from Buddhism:

The 'Dual' in the Nondual

Vedanta:

Dvaita and Advaita,

The Born in the Unborn,

Maya and Brahman,

The Unreal in the Real.

Judaism:

The Created and Jehovah,

Existence in 'The Ground' (of existence),

The Sefirot and the Ein-Sof,

The Manifest in the Unmanifest.

Christianity:

The Son and the Father,

The 'Known' in the Unknown,

The Caused and the 'First Cause',

The Moved and the 'Prime Mover'.

Islam:

The Muslim and Allah,

The Witnessed and the Witness,

The Sufi and Fana,

The 'Self' in the Non-Self.

Hinduism:

Sakti and Siva,

Consciousness in Motion and at Rest,

Kali and Om,

That which Appears/Exists/Disappears in Pure Awareness,

The Lila and the Nitya,

The Seen in the Unseen.

Buddhism:

Samsara and Nirvana,

The Ephemeral in the Eternal,

The Plenum and Sunyata (the void),

The Perceived in the Imperceptible,

Nirmanakaya and Dharmakaya,

The Limited in the Unlimited.

Glossary

Advaita: non-dual.

Brahman: the all-pervading transcendental Absolute Reality.

Dharmakaya: the Absolute Unmanifest Reality that is 'Aware Nothingness'.

Dvaita: dualist school of Vedantic philosophy proposed by Madhva.

Ein sof (or *En-Sof*): the infinite nothingness, the source and final resting place of all things.

Fana: absorption into the Absolute, which al-Junaid of Baghdad interpreted as 'dying to self'.

Kali: the Divine Mother, creator, preserver and destroyer. Sakti, cosmic energy, consciousness in motion.

Lila: the divine play or manifestation, consciousness in motion.

Maya: the power of Brahman, which supports the cosmic illusion of the One appearing as the many.

Nirmanakaya: the dimension of ceaseless manifestation, or the compassionate energy of Rigpa.

Nirvana: Buddhist word for *moksa*, enlightenment, awakening.

Nitya: the Ultimate Reality, the eternal Absolute.

Om: Brahman 'The Impersonal Absolute'; but is also the Logos, The Word, in the 'Ground of Being', in which all manifestation arises, exists and subsides.

Plenum: a space filled with matter, or the whole of space so regarded (OED).

Rigpa: pure awareness which is 'the nature of everything'.

Sakti: cosmic energy, consciousness in motion.

Samsara: the wheel of birth, life, death and rebirth.

Sefirot: the stages of divine being and aspects of divine personality.

Siva: universal consciousness when it is at rest, aware of every movement occurring in it, which is 'pure awareness'.

Sunyata: the void, formless awareness, aware nothingness.

Chapter Sixteen

Instrument of The Absolute

This chapter shows how investigation of experience can reveal living organisms to be instruments of The Absolute, by which This can 'know' Itself.

Instruments of The Absolute

If you sit quietly noticing the sensations in (and on the surface of) your body, you can easily see that these occur, are detected by the nervous system and then appear in awareness, i.e. you become aware of them.

In the same vein you can notice that sounds occur, are detected by the ears, and then appear in awareness.

Sights occur, are detected by the eyes, and then appear in awareness.

Aromas occur, are detected by the nose, and then appear in awareness.

Flavours occur, are detected by the taste buds and then appear in awareness.

Thoughts occur, are detected by the mind, and then appear in awareness.

Mental images occur, are detected by the mind, and then appear in awareness.

Therefore the physical mind/body is an instrument through which awareness (consciousness at rest) can sense and contemplate the physical manifestation of cosmic energy (consciousness in motion, or motion in consciousness).

So the body/mind is an instrument through which awareness can experience the physical world, for experience *is* awareness of thoughts/mental images/sensations.

The body/mind is also an instrument through which awareness can interact with, and enjoy, the universal manifestation of cosmic energy.

Thus the body/mind is an instrument through which consciousness can 'know itself' when manifest as the physical world, that is when in motion.

The human mind has the added advantage of being capable of 'self realization' that is of realizing the deeper level of 'pure awareness', consciousness at rest, the unmanifest.

Instruments of The Absolute

Therefore the human mind/body is an instrument through which consciousness can 'know itself' in both 'modes': at rest and in motion. That is as pure awareness and as the physical universe.

This realization of humans as instruments of the divine (consciousness) occurs in many of the world's religions. In Judaism, as instruments to enjoy and continue the creation; in Islam, as instruments through which Allah could know Himself; in Advaita Vedanta, as instruments through which Brahman could know Himself and His manifestation; and in Vaishnavism, as instruments to perform Yagnas (sacrifices) for the satisfaction of Krishna (Vishnu). There are also echoes of this in Christianity where man can be seen as an instrument to glorify God and receive His benefits. Mahayana Buddhism also has the concept of the Bodhisattva as an instrument to work for the enlightenment of all beings.

This is particularly stressed in Advaita Vedanta where we find the idea delineated in the Upanishads:

> As Brahman is everything, it follows that we all are
> Brahman and that He is the agent by which the mind

thinks, eye sees, tongue speaks, ear hears and body breathes (*Kena* I v.5-9). He is also described as the 'ear of the ear, eye of the eye, mind of the mind, word of the words and life of the life' (*Kena* I v.2). Thus He is the pure awareness (*Brihadaranyaka* 4 v.7) in which all thought, life and sensation appears; and He is the 'seer' (*Isha* v.8) and 'all knowing' (*Katha* 2 v.18). [31]

The Katha Upanishad likens man to a chariot, of which the atman (the Self, awareness, Brahman within each individual) is the master, the body is the chariot, the mind is the charioteer, the sense organs are the horses and the roads they travel on are the objects of sensation. The atman is the enjoyer and experiencer of the ride, which is made possible by the charioteer, chariot and horses. (Katha Upanishad 3v.3-4) So Brahman needs the mind and senses, to enjoy and experience the physical world. However, when the mind is unaware of the master's presence, through lack of discrimination, it is unable to control the senses which run amok like wild horses (Ibid 3v.5). Brahman, pure consciousness, is hidden in every heart, being the eternal witness watching everything one does. He is said to be 'the operator'

---

[31] C. Drake, *Beyond The Separate Self,* 2009, Halifax, p.136.

whilst we are his 'innumerable instruments'. (Svetasvetara Upanishad 6v.10-12) [32]

Moreover, it is not only humans but all 'sensing' organisms that are instruments through which consciousness can 'know itself' when manifest as the physical world, that is when in motion. Obviously different organisms have different capacities in this respect as all senses are limited to certain wavelengths, or range, of sensation (experience). As far as we know humans are the only species capable of 'self realization' that is of realizing the deeper level of 'pure awareness', consciousness at rest, and thus are the only beings through which consciousness can 'know itself' when at rest as pure awareness. However, there could well be other species, terrestrial and non-terrestrial, that are capable of this. Humans are also only limited instruments in terms of sensing, contemplating and 'knowing' the manifest and the unmanifest.

---

[32] C. Drake, *Humanity Our Place in the Universe*, 2010, Halifax, p.55.

Chapter Seventeen

Purpose and Meaning

This chapter deals with purpose and meaning, and attempts to show that it is only when identified as a separate individual, living in an alien world, that life seems meaningless unless it is given an extrinsic 'purpose'.

Purpose and Meaning

In this chapter I shall discuss Hindu cosmology and its divine 'plan', although 'play' would be more appropriate. I shall then consider whether this gives life a purpose or makes it meaningful. I will attempt to show that when one engages totally in this 'play' life becomes so enjoyable and pleasurable that no other purpose is necessary, and that this joy and pleasure gives subjective meaning to one's existence. I shall also try to demonstrate that all life has objective meaning whether the life form in question is aware of this or not. Finally, I shall consider some objections that could be raised for such a view and offer counters to them.

For me the most plausible divine plan/purpose rests in Hindu cosmology. In this, Brahman (the totality of cosmic power, energy, consciousness and awareness) rests as a single point before the creation of the universe. Compare this to the 'singularity' which modern physics/astronomy posits existed before the 'big bang'. From Brahman is manifested the universe and he pervades it, or dwells in it as it. In The Tattirya Upanishad we find:

The Lord of Love (Brahman) willed: "Let there be many!"
> He who has no form assumed many forms;
> He who is infinite appeared finite;

> He who is everywhere assumed a place;
> He who is all wisdom caused ignorance;
> He who is real caused unreality.
> It is He who gives reality to all.
> Before the universe was created,
> Brahman existed as unmanifest.
> (Taittiriya Upanishad Part II 6.1-7.1)[33]

Brahman is considered to have two aspects: the witnessing/awareness aspect (consciousness at rest) and cosmic energy, which is the aspect of creation, preservation and destruction (motion in consciousness). Every 'thing' that is occurring in consciousness is a manifestation of cosmic energy, for the string theory[34] and the earlier theory of relativity show that matter is in fact energy, which is motion in consciousness. For energy is synonymous with motion and consciousness is the substratum, or deepest level, of all existence.

Now all motion arises in stillness, exists in stillness, is known by its comparison with stillness, and eventually subsides back into stillness. For example, if you walk across a room, before you

---

[33] E. Easwaran, *The Upanishads*, 1988, Penguin, New Delhi, p.143
[34] This posits that all 'things' are composed of 'strings' of energy in complex configurations, vibrating at various frequencies.

start there is stillness, as you walk the room is still and you know you are moving relative to this stillness, and when you stop once again there is stillness. In the same way every 'thing' (motion in consciousness) arises in awareness (consciousness at rest), exists in awareness, is known in awareness and subsides back into awareness. Awareness is still, but is the container of all potential energy which is continually bubbling up into manifestation (physical energy) and then subsiding back into stillness.

Thus there is no dichotomy or duality between the physical world and 'awareness' for they are both manifestations of the same essence. The physical universe is just cosmic energy (motion in consciousness) when it is manifest into physical form, and awareness (consciousness at rest) contains this same energy in latent form as potential energy.

This explains the cosmology, but what of plan or purpose? According to the Hindus this is all the *lila* (play) of Brahman in the aspect of creation, preservation and destruction, which some call the 'Divine Mother'. This 'play' is purely for her enjoyment:

> The Divine Mother is always playful and sportive. The universe is her play. ... She wants to continue playing

> with her created beings. ... Her pleasure is in continuing the game.[35]

Before we can consider whether this makes our lives as human beings meaningful, we have to consider what we really are. Are we just puppets who are being played with by some divine force, or manifestations of that force participating fully in the 'play'? According to the Hindus Brahman is the container of the universe and also what is contained in it. Thus we are, in essence, also 'That' (Brahman) and able to participate fully in the 'play'.

However, this is not possible whist we consider ourselves as separate individual beings trying to make our way in an alien world. This is mainly because this stops us 'being' the present moment and engaging totally in the 'play'. Consider the play of children who totally lose themselves in the game and thus participate fully with maximum enjoyment. As long as we consider ourselves to be a separate ego we are always trying to better ourselves, achieve more (knowledge, possessions, power, fame etc.), polish our self-image and generally build ourselves up. This tends to make us live in the future and stops us living fully in the present moment. The other side of this coin is to live in regret

---

[35] S.Nikhilananda, *'The Gospel of Sri Ramakrishna'*, 1942, Chennai, p. 136

Purpose and Meaning

as to what might have been, self-loathing, melancholy or yearning for the past. This also stops us seeing 'what is' here and now, either by making us live in the past or by the mind spinning on our failures and lack of self-worth.

I realize that this goes against modern western thought which finds meaning in achievement/purpose rather than the sheer enjoyment of 'what is' at any given moment. Consider the following quotes from *The Meaning of Life*:

> What counts is that one should be able to begin a new task, a new castle, a new bubble.[36] (Richard Taylor)

> In so far as I have carved out my being in the human world, I go on existing in the future. [37] (Hazel Barnes)

I am not suggesting that having and achieving goals is not a source of great satisfaction, but it does not compare to the bliss evoked when one comes across a stunning sunset which is seen with a still mind, or when you are at a concert and you hear the music so deeply that you 'become' the music. This occurs when

---

[36] E. D. Klemke, *The Meaning of Life*, 2000, Oxford, p. 175
[37] Ibid. p. 166

Purpose and Meaning

you totally 'lose yourself' in the manifestation. The point here is that the world is a wonderful place when seen 'as it is' with a still mind and no reference to a separate individual seer. In other words when it is seen in its actual reality and not through the narrow filter of the mind's likes/dislikes, judgements and opinions. I can offer no proof of this apart from the fact that it is my experience and has also been pointed to by many mystics, past and present. This can, in fact, only be known through experience and not through reason and the intellect.

Why should this be the case? Our deeper level of pure awareness, an aspect of Brahman, is who we 'are' at a deeper level than mind/body. Our mind/bodies are the instruments with which It (as we) senses and 'plays in' Its creation. Thus when you filter any sensation through the mind you are 'colouring' it with something less (the mind's likes/dislikes, opinions and judgements) than the pure awareness in which it appears, and so masking its actual reality.

How does this makes life seem meaningful to me, and could any other considerations bring this into doubt?

Purpose and Meaning

A common definition of meaningful is "full of significance or importance" and from this we can also derive the idea of 'being valuable'. So when one feels that one's experiences, activities and aspirations are important, significant or valuable one finds life meaningful. It can also be argued that life is objectively meaningful, if it is valuable, whether one feels it to be so or not.

What makes life meaningful to me has two components: subjective which makes my life seem and feel worth living and objective which makes my life, and indeed all life, meaningful. First I need to discuss my view of 'life', both mine and in general. This can be seen to agree with the Hindu view given before, but it is not just a belief system as it has been realized through direct investigation of reality and the nature of experience.

After many years of search, meditation and contemplation I have realized, and experienced, that there exists an omnipresent 'field' of pure consciousness and energy. Everything in manifestation appears in this 'field', exists in this 'field' and upon dissolution, merges back into this 'field'. Compare this to the 'unified field theory' which has been the 'holy grail' of modern physics since Einstein first proposed it. Indeed the 'string theory', which is gaining prominence, proposes that everything in existence is composed purely of myriad 'strings' of energy. Even under the older model Einstein showed that matter was equivalent to energy and thus the Universe could be considered to be composed purely of energy.

Thus 'I' am purely an expression of this 'field' and indeed not separate from it. I have appeared in it, exist in it (and am fully dependent on it) and upon my death will merge back into it. On the physical level this is obvious for the body, whilst living, is totally dependent on its environment for the food, water and air it requires to live, and on dying it breaks down into the chemical elements/compounds from which it is constituted.

On the mental/spiritual level it can be realized by sitting quietly and noticing that:

>   There is effortless consciousness of every thought.
>   There is effortless consciousness of every sound.
>   There is effortless consciousness of every sight.
>   There is effortless consciousness of every taste.
>   There is effortless consciousness of every smell.
>   There is effortless consciousness of every feeling.
>   There is effortless consciousness of every touch.

Purpose and Meaning

This consciousness is effortless and choiceless as it is effortlessly and choicelessly present and precedes every thought and sensation. That is to say that this is always present and as soon as a thought/sensation occurs there is consciousness of it.

For each of us this consciousness is omnipresent. If you investigate you will find that it is (and has been) always present wherever you are. Even during sleep there is consciousness of dreams, and of the quality of that sleep. There is also consciousness of sensations for if a sensation becomes strong enough (such as a sound or discomfort) it will wake you up.

Every mind/body experience appears in this consciousness, exists in this consciousness, is seen by this consciousness and disappears back into this consciousness.

In fact this consciousness encompasses every mind/body experience and deeper than this ever changing mind/body you are this consciousness

Purpose and Meaning

This can also be backed up by the following argument: In any experience there are only three things, or classes of things: physical sensations, mental activity and 'consciousness' of physical sensations/mental activity. This 'consciousness' contains physical sensations/mental activity (mind/body), for they appear in it, i.e. as soon as you experience any physical sensation/mental activity it appears in consciousness and you can 'become aware' of it (i.e. see it with the mind). This 'consciousness', the receptacle of all physical sensation/mental activity, is an aspect of the 'Totality' (the field) of energy and consciousness, and is who (or what) we are at a deeper level than mind/body.

One counter argument to this is that if we 'become aware' of physical/sensations, mental activity, in the 'totality of consciousness' why can we not 'become aware' of other people's physical sensations/mental activity. I posit that this is, in general, because our mind only has access to that portion of consciousness in which our mind/body's sensations are appearing. Rather like the way in which a program executing on a computer is located in RAM but only has access to that portion of RAM in which it, and its buffer, are located. However, considering Jung's theory of the 'collective sub-conscious' (archetypes) and Rupert Sheldrake's theory of 'morphic resonance' there is some evidence that it is possible for the human mind to have access to all knowledge that exists in consciousness

I realize that this view is open to question but it is how I experience life. This leads me to attempt to live life totally in the present moment, without reference to the past and future, and to experience the world 'as it is' without reference to an individual, separate 'seer'. This is because the past is gone, leaving no impression and I have no concern for the future as I am just part of the whole ('field') and not a separate individual struggling to make his way in an 'alien' world. It is interesting to note that Albert Camus, as he began to realize that the world is not infused with 'human values' began to find it alien and hostile. This is because, when one is identified as a human (mind/body) one is not identified with the 'Totality', of which the world is a manifestation, and thus one feels that the world is 'alien' and 'hostile'. In fact, of course, the world is anything but that, as it provides everything our mind/bodies need for their existence!

When one lives life moment to moment, without reference to an individual 'seer', there are daily occurrences of great wonder, beauty, awe and gratitude (for life). This is because when experienced without reference to the past/future all experiences are new and fresh and thus things perceived as 'through the eyes of a child'. Also when not referenced to an individual seer, i.e. not filtered through the mind's labelling, likes/dislikes, opinions and prejudices, things are seen 'as they are' with a still mind. When nature is seen 'as it is' it is much brighter, more vivid, more stunning than when seen through the mind's filter.

So these moments of great wonder, beauty, awe and gratitude are like bright 'jewels' that illuminate my life and I value them very highly. This is not to say that I grasp them and try to hold them, for this is once again misidentifying as a separate being, but I enjoy them 'moment to moment' as they come and go. So these valuable experiences are part of what makes my life seem meaningful.

The other main factor is the realization that we are all expressions of this 'Totality' (field) of consciousness and energy. As such we are all essentially the same and there is, in reality, no separation between us. This realization naturally leads to treating one's neighbour as oneself. In fact once one has discovered that one is just part of the 'Totality' this leads to the end of all psychological suffering caused by identifying oneself with a mind, body, or self-image. This purely imaginary 'self-image' causes much of our psychological suffering; for with no self-image, but just being 'moment to moment', there is no fear of losing face, of not achieving or of failure, as there is nothing (no self-image) to nurture, build-up or protect. Once this is realized, and you see all of the unnecessary psychological suffering around you, the natural tendency is to attempt to alleviate this by pointing out to as many people as possible this simple truth, that they are not just mind/bodies, that any 'self-image' is an illusion, and that they are part of (and expressions of) the Totality (field) of consciousness and energy. The attempt to do this, which I consider to be a very valuable endeavour, is the other main thing that gives my life subjective meaning.

Moving on to objective meaning, this is to do with the plan or purpose of creation, or the universe.

According to this the 'Totality' (Brahman) intentionally manifested itself into the whole of creation for its own entertainment and enjoyment. I suggest that in the same way that we use a computer (and all of its multimedia functionality) and the internet as an instrument to sense and experience the world around us, so the 'Totality' uses our body/minds, instrumentally, to sense, experience, and enjoy the universe. This topic is the focus of the previous chapter 'Instruments of the Absolute'.

So 'my life', when related to the body/mind, means that period of time when the 'Totality' (as me) uses this body/mind to sense and experience its creation. Thus this body/mind has extrinsic, or instrumental, value and its existence is valuable or meaningful irrespective of what I do! This applies to all of my activities as they are experienced by not only my mind/body but also the 'Totality' of consciousness in which they appear. I hasten to add that this does not give me carte-blanche to do whatever I may feel like irrespective of its effect on other beings. This is because, in essence, all beings are part of the 'Totality' and thus there is in reality no separation (between them and me).

As far as harming their external manifestation (mind/bodies) in any way, they are also instruments and should be respected as such. This brings me to the point that all lives are valuable, and therefore meaningful, in the same way that mine is, in that all body/minds are extrinsically valuable as instruments of the 'Totality'. Thus all life is meaningful, in its own way, whether the particular life-form in question is aware of this or not.

Purpose and Meaning

Finally, consider the problems that this view encounters. The first, and for the philosopher the main, problem is that it cannot be proved by argument and reason. In fact these are the tools which obscure it. It has to be experienced, but for this you have to know, existentially, that you are not separate from 'That', the totality of being. Unfortunately, this knowledge is impossible to obtain as long as you identify with the mind/body or as a separate individual. In this state one overlooks the pure joy and pleasure of living moment to moment and tends to feel that:

> Whenever we are…directed back to existence itself we are overtaken by its worthlessness and vanity and this is … called boredom.[38] (Schopenhauer)

This is because we are identifying with our rational mind and using it to judge every moment, rather than just 'being' with a still mind and experiencing the actual reality of existence.

Albert Camus unknowingly puts his finger on the exact problem when he says:

---

[38] E. D. Klemke, *The Meaning of Life*, 2000, Oxford p. 69

> Thinking of the future, establishing aims for oneself, having preferences ... presupposes a belief in freedom. ... But that freedom to 'be' which alone can serve as a basis for truth does not exist.[39]

The point is that pure 'being' can only be experienced when one is not 'thinking of the future, establishing aims and having preferences'; the two states are mutually exclusive, the second preventing the first!

Summing up: when one lives moment to moment, identified with the 'totality of being', one is able to engage fully in the 'Divine Play'. This makes life light, not heavy, and thoroughly enjoyable not requiring any extrinsic purpose. This joy gives life subjective meaning, and indeed all lives are objectively meaningful as they have instrumental value to the Totality of being, energy and consciousness. It is only when identified as a separate individual, living in an alien world, that life seems meaningless unless it is given an extrinsic purpose.

---

[39] Ibid. p. 99

Chapter Eighteen

On This and That

An expanded version of the poem from *Beyond the Separate Self*, with additional commentary, that sums it all up.

'That which you already are, pure awareness' – *Sogyal Rinpoche*

'Awareness of awareness – the first factor of enlightenment' – *The Buddha*

'Effortless Choiceless Awareness is our Real State' – *Sri Ramana Maharshi*

On This and That

Overcome fear ... by seeing what's Here!

Let go of all fear and anxiety, for awareness is always present as you are effortlessly, and choicelessly, aware of your thoughts and sensations. This awareness is a constant subjective presence, whereas these thoughts and sensations (mind/body) are ephemeral objects coming and going within this awareness. Therefore this awareness is the deepest level of our being, the unchanging presence that we intuitively feel we are and have always been, that which has never been absent and has witnessed the pantomime of our lives. This very awareness, the home which we have never left, and can in fact never leave, is the very peace and security that we seek.

Forget about church ... Just give up the search!

To enjoy this peace and absolute security we do not need any dogma, belief systems, rituals or practices. All that is necessary is to abandon the external search for this. We must stop 'looking for love in all the wrong places'; just recognize, and totally relax into, that pure awareness that we already are.

No need for a prayer mat... Already you are That!

For this to occur there is no need to appeal to any external deity, for this awareness is itself the 'hidden treasure', the Absolute Reality lauded by all religions, and is always present at the deeper (and surface) level of our being. At the deeper level as That in which thoughts/sensations (mind/body) appear/disappear, come and go, arise and subside; and at the surface level as this very awareness of these thoughts/sensations.

No Me, No you! There's nothing to do...

In reality there is no separate individual entity (me or you) we are both just expressions of the same pure awareness, and there's nothing we need to do to achieve enlightenment as we are already 'That', i.e. awareness is already present.

Nobody, No mind! There's nothing to find....

There is, in reality, nobody, i.e. separate individual; and no entity called the mind which is just a flow of ephemeral thoughts and images. There is also nothing to find in that we cannot lose that pure awareness that, in essence, we always are; we just need to stop overlooking this.

No effort, No sweat! There's nothing to get....

There is no need to make any effort to achieve enlightenment, just stop and turn your attention to that pure awareness that you already are. You cannot 'get' this as you already 'are' this!

Wow! There's only Now…

In reality there is always only now as the past has already gone and the future is yet to be. If you see 'what is' in the 'now' with no reference to past (including acquired knowledge or imaginary 'individual self') or future, then everything seems much more vivid and alive (Wow!) than when filtered through the mind and its opinions, judgments, attitudes and 'knowledge'.

Cheer! There's only Here…

Also you are always 'Here', at any given moment, and can only see 'what is' here (and now). What you think is going on anywhere else is only speculation, which will take you away from the direct experience of 'here and now'.

How? Just Here and Now!

How to be 'enlightened' (i.e. unburdened) and at peace? Just be totally here in the present moment and see 'what is' (here and now) with no reference to the past, future, mind, or what might be happening anywhere else.

Just This! That's Bliss....

This seeing 'what is' with a still mind, from pure awareness, is Bliss. The other name for Brahman (The Absolute) is Satchitananda which can be translated as: 'What is', the awareness of 'What is', the Bliss of the awareness of 'What is'.

Just Cease! That's Peace...

Just cease identifying with the mind (and all of its activity to get anywhere, or attain anything) and the result is instant peace.

Just Being! That's freeing......

.

Just 'Being' moment to moment, with no reference to past/future or any illusory separate 'self', is in itself totally freeing…

Accept what is … Then feel the kiss!

Always accept 'what is' at the present moment with no resistance and life becomes more enjoyable as the mind stills. This does not mean that we cannot plan to change things, only that we need to accept 'what is Now' as it is already here and therefore cannot be changed. This lack of resistance liberates tremendous energy, and relaxation, allowing us to 'feel the kiss', and wonder, of Reality.

Live with no 'story'… Then all reveals its glory!

If you live life with no personal 'story' then the mind stills and everything in manifestation appears more vivid and alive, i.e. more glorious…

Each moment is enough… The end of all Stuff!

If you check you will find that Pure Awareness never needs anything to change and is complete whatever is happening. In this 'each moment is enough' and no mind activity is necessary to change, or seek for, anything.

On This and That

Overcome fear … by seeing what's Here!

Forget about church … Just give up the search!

No need for a prayer mat... Already you are That!

No Me, No you! There's nothing to do...

Nobody, No mind! There's nothing to find....

No effort, No sweat! There's nothing to get....

Wow! There's only Now…

Cheer! There's only Here…

How? Just Here and Now!

Just This! That's Bliss....

Just Cease! That's Peace...

Just Being! That's freeing.......

Accept what is … Then feel the kiss!

Live with no 'story'… Then all reveals its glory!

Each moment is enough… The end of all Stuff!

Chapter Nineteen

Nothing Has Essential Meaning

This chapter investigates whether anything has essential meaning. That is whether any 'thing' has meaning with regard to our essential identity, who or what we are. It also addresses the major human problem of 'reading meaning into things that have no meaning' In addition there is a discussion about the essential meaning of nothingness.

Nothing Has Essential Meaning

There are two definitions of this to consider: no 'thing' has meaning (significance), and nothing (ness) has meaning (is significant).

<u>No 'thing' has meaning.</u>

Within this I am going to consider whether any thing has ultimate (absolute) meaning and whether any thing has existential meaning, that is whether any thing has significance regarding who, or what, we 'are'. I am not going to consider whether any thing has subjective meaning, that is at the level of body/mind where we all have things that we consider to be significant.

At the Absolute, or Ultimate, level all things are just manifestations of cosmic energy, which is consciousness in motion (or motion in consciousness). They arise in and from awareness (consciousness at rest), exist in this, are 'seen' by this, and subside back into this. Therefore no thing has lasting existence or significance and thus no ultimate meaning; although, as previously discussed, living organisms do have temporary value (meaning) as instruments through which consciousness can 'know itself'.

Nothing Has Essential Meaning

At the existential level whether any thing has any meaning depends on what we identify ourselves as (being). There are many things that people regard as being meaningful in this respect, in my case for instance:

> I am a double Taurus, with Sagittarius rising.
> I am a (was born in the year of the) Rat.
> I am a number seven.
> I am a number nine in the enneagram
> I am an English Australian.
> I am middle class.
> I am a Hindu/Buddhist/Christian Yogi.
> I am a sixty three year old white anglo-saxon male.
> I am a potter.
> I am a writer.
> I am a father and husband.
> I am in good health.
> I am a meditator and investigator.
> I am (was, not now) a spiritual seeker.
> I am (was, not now) a vegetarian.
> I am (was, not now) a renunciate.

Nothing Has Essential Meaning

These are all examples of things we are told could mean something about us. Now these may, or may not, say something about our personality but do they really say anything about us as we really are? If we misidentify at the surface level of body/mind, and thus the ego, they all seem to have significance. However, then each of these just adds another level of misidentification and gives us a more concrete feeling of being a personality.

At the deeper level of pure awareness these are obviously meaningless, as at this level I do not exist as a separate being, so that any assertion that 'I am …anything' is not only meaningless but is also false. Though such thoughts may appear interesting at the surface level of body/mind they need to held in this context and to be regarded as essentially meaningless. So if, for instance, one has an astrological chart/reading done this is to be considered to be pure entertainment (as is life as it happens) and not to be saying anything about who (or what) one truly is. As Nisargadatta said: 'All these activities go on, but they are only entertainment.'[40]

Reading meaning into things that have no meaning has caused much human misery over the millennia. Most wars are fought in

[40] http://nisargadatta.co.cc/pages/quotes_consciousness_and_absolute.html

such meaningless causes as nationalism, religion, tribalism, racism etc... All of which have no essential meaning. That is not to say that the world's religions do not point to essential meaning, but which religion you follow does not make you a member of an exclusive group which is superior to other beings. It is amazing how humanity is prepared to die for and kill in defence of, or propagation of, an idea or false sense of identity with an exclusive group ... both of which are essentially meaningless!

Even at the level of day to day living 'reading meaning into things that have no meaning' limits the lives of many people. This is a major factor in most mental illnesses and we all engage in it one way or another when we let trivial things affect our equanimity. For instance, if I get depressed when the soccer team I support keeps losing ... which it does! Now this obviously has no meaning apart from the fact that this football team is not very good, but if I identify myself as being a supporter of that team then I can infer that their ineptitude says something about me ... Also most people are superstitious to one degree or another and 'reading meaning into things that have no meaning' is obviously the cause of all superstition. Imagine how freeing it would be if one could truly see things as they 'are' and not ascribe any fictitious meaning to them! The easiest way to achieve this is by experientially discovering the deeper level of pure awareness and identifying with this.

Nothing has meaning.

Everything that we experience, that is all thoughts, mental images, and sensations can only be noticed relative to the 'nothingness' in which they appear. Consider the following:

> When we look at any form (thing) we see this form in contrast to the space that surrounds it, without which we would not be able to see it. Consider a marble statue sculpted from a single block of stone. The statue only appears as the stone is chipped away, leaving the space that envelops the form. Before the sculptor begins, the form already potentially exists in the block of stone, but this only becomes apparent when the space in which it exists is exposed. Similarly *all* sensations are only known in contrast to the nothingness in which they occur and appear. Sounds, for example, are only known (heard) relative to the silence that surrounds them. If there is no silence, then either the sound is not heard, or it is muffled or distorted. For instance, if a bird is singing at 40

decibels and a lawn mower is being operated at 80 decibels you will not hear the bird. As soon as the mower is switched off the bird song is immediately heard within the silence that envelops it.[41]

And taking this further:

There is awareness of all thoughts relative to the silence (no thought) in which they appear, exist and subside.

There is awareness of all bodily feelings relative to the neutrality (lack of feeling) in which they appear, exist and subside.

There is awareness of all sounds relative to the silence in which they appear, exist and subside.

There is awareness of all forms (things seen) relative to the space (formlessness) in which they appear, exist and subside.

---

[41] C. Drake, *Beyond the Separate Self*, 2009, Halifax, p.81

Nothing Has Essential Meaning

There is awareness of all odours relative to the odourlessness in which they appear, exist and subside.

There is awareness of all flavours (tastes) relative to the neutrality (lack of flavour) in which they appear, exist and subside.

As the only things in our direct experience are thoughts (including all mental images) and sensations, awareness of which is only possible due to contrast with the 'nothingness' in which they appear, then this 'nothingness' is absolutely vital for awareness of any 'thing', and is in fact a property of awareness itself.[42]

Moreover, awareness is consciousness at rest which implies 'nothingness' as all 'things' are manifestations of cosmic energy and thus in movement. Every 'thing' (consciousness in motion) arises in awareness (consciousness at rest), exists in awareness, is known in awareness and subsides back into awareness. Awareness is still, but is the container of all potential energy which is continually bubbling up into manifestation (physical energy … 'things') and then subsiding back into stillness.

---

[42] C. Drake, *Beyond the Separate Self*, 2009, Halifax, p. 69-70

Nothing Has Essential Meaning

Therefore 'nothingness' has meaning and significance as a property of awareness, the container of all 'things' and as the background relative to which 'things' may be seen.

Chapter Twenty

Free Will … Myth or Reality?

This chapter discusses the question of whether we have free will.

Existentialism posits that 'existence precedes essence' maintaining that we 'make ourselves the individuals we are'; which Sartre interpreted as 'we are what we choose ourselves to be'.[43] This philosophy obviously considers that each human has free will to determine its own 'essence'.

In comparison most religions would maintain the opposite: that 'essence precedes existence', which means that God, The Absolute, is the 'essence' of all creation and thus precedes the existence of all 'things'. Some would argue that The Absolute must exist and this 'existence therefore precedes essence'; however, for the consideration of whether humans have free will this is irrelevant.

According to these religions humans have no free will to determine their 'essence', as this has already been determined by the Absolute and is impervious to human manipulation. This is the question that this essay is to consider, whether humans have free will to determine their 'essence'.

Some determinists go even further than religions in maintaining that humans have absolutely no free will at all and that all of our

---

[43] T. Hondercih, *The Oxford Companion to Philosophy*, 2005, Oxford, p.277.

actions are governed by our genes, upbringing, conditioning and subconscious. However, this is outside the scope of this essay which deals only with 'free will and essence'. Personally I (at the surface level ... see later) regard this concept as absurd, which can easily be negated by tossing a coin in making small decisions (we have no control over the result, but we did choose to toss a coin) or deliberately choosing to override one's natural 'choice' occasionally. These actions may go 'against the grain' but the very fact that one can carry them out proves that one has free will to do so.

So let us consider the two propositions that: 'existence precedes essence' and its antonym 'essence precedes existence'. Interestingly both can be supported by the Oxford English Dictionary, which gives two definitions for 'essence':

> The intrinsic nature or indispensable quality of something, which determines its nature.

> A property, or group of properties, of something without which it would not exist or be what it is.[44]

---

[44] *Compact Oxford Dictionary*, 2005, Oxford, p.488.

Free Will ... Myth or Reality?

So if you believe that 'existence precedes essence' then you believe that you have free will to change your intrinsic nature by developing, or changing, your indispensable quality or properties that 'make you what you are'. The credo is: 'Because I exist I can manifest my own essence'. Thus one has free will to determine one's own essence.

However, if you believe that 'essence precedes existence' then you believe that your 'intrinsic nature' and your very existence stem from your essence. The credo here is: 'I am a manifestation of my essence and thus am unable to change it'. Thus one's essence is predetermined and one has no free will to influence it.

The basic difference here comes down to self-identity ... 'what am I' in essence?
In the first case I am an existing thing (separate object) and therefore can change my essence.
In the second I am a manifestation of my essence which I am therefore unable to change.

As an example of these views I am going to consider the materialist view, I am the mind/body, and the Vedantic (Nondual) view, I am pure consciousness of which my mind/body is a manifestation.

In the materialist view my essence is a 'separate self' identified as: my thoughts and sensations, personality and self-image consisting of my physical appearance, mental ability, status, occupation, position in society, family situation, achievements, lack of achievements, ambitions, hopes, fears, memories and projections into the future. Thus I have free will to change these and therefore my essence.

In the nondual view there exists universal consciousness (pure awareness, the constant conscious subjective presence that 'sees' all of our thoughts/sensations) totally at rest, completely still, aware of everything that is occurring within it. Every 'thing' that is occurring in consciousness is a manifestation of cosmic energy, for the string theory[45] and the earlier theory of relativity show that matter is in fact energy, which is consciousness in motion (or motion in consciousness). For energy is synonymous with motion and consciousness is the substratum, or deepest level, of

---

[45] This posits that all 'things' are composed of 'strings' of energy in complex configurations, vibrating at various frequencies.

all existence. Thus I am purely a manifestation of this essence and have no free will to change it.

In fact with this view I do not exist as a separate person (object) but am always just an ephemeral manifestation of consciousness itself, and therefore cannot possibly have any personal free will!

From my point of view we just need to consider the last of the eight points mentioned in chapter eleven:

> This does not mean that at a surface level we are not the mind and body, for they arise in, are perceived by and subside back into awareness, which is the deepest and most fundamental level of our being. However, if we choose to identify with this deepest level – awareness – (the perceiver) rather than the surface level, mind/body (the perceived), then thoughts and sensations are seen for what they truly are, just ephemeral objects which come and go, leaving awareness itself totally unaffected.[46]

Thus in this view whilst we are awareness, or consciousness, at the deepest level and have no free will, we are also mind/body at

---

[46] C. Drake, *Beyond the Separate Self*, 2009, Halifax, p.18-20.

the surface level. If we identify with this level then we, as previously discussed, seem to have free will. This is the case until we finally realize the deeper level, that is the essence, of our being. So we have free will to realize our essence, but this realization also includes the realization of no free will, for at this level the seemingly separate person has ceased to exist as an object!

So when, in *Beyond the Separate Self*, I say:

> At this stage one needs to come to a decision about which one values more: the objective level of thoughts and sensations or the deeper subjective peaceful level of pure awareness.[47]

This is the view from the surface level, where we have the free will to 'make this decision'; for at the deeper level the realization has become already established and there is no one to make any decision!

---

[47] C. Drake, *Beyond the Separate Self*, 2009, Halifax, p.98.

Free Will ... Myth or Reality?

Summing up when one is identified as a body/mind it appears as if 'existence precedes essence' and one has free will. If one uses this free will to develop 'understanding which comes with alert perceptivity, eager enquiry and deep investigation'[48] and discover the deeper level of pure awareness then one realizes that 'essence precedes existence'. With this realization the mind/body is seen to be just an ephemeral manifestation of pure consciousness and free will is seen to be an illusion.

---

[48] Nisargadatta, *I Am That*, 1997, Durham NY, p. 534.

Chapter Twenty One

The Practical Application of Awakening

This chapter attempts to debunk the myth that awakening can be detrimental to one's ability to cope with day to day life in the world.

'By observing mental states you also become aware of the seven factors of enlightenment [awakening]. These are: **awareness of awareness**, **investigation of the Way**, vigour, joy, serenity, concentration and equanimity.' (The Buddha, Maha Sattipatthana Sutta 14-16)

The first two are paramount and the last five are outcomes of these. This is what my book *Beyond the Separate Self* is all about, becoming 'aware of awareness' through direct investigation and then continuing with further 'investigation of the Way' (the Tao, the nature of reality). Once one is 'aware of awareness' then one can undertake further investigations not needing to relying on any teachings, although these may be useful for confirming what one has discovered. These investigations lead to awakening, but many people question the usefulness of this in helping us to live in the world.

My neighbour is the sole carer of three young children. Consequently he finds life very hard and, having had two children of my own, I can fully sympathize with his plight. However, this is not very helpful. For us to sit together and agree how difficult such a situation is will not improve things. It will only strengthen his opinion of the problems of raising three infants and increase his desperation. The negative mind state can only be strengthened by other's sympathy, for this fuels one's justification for feeling this way.

What is required is a paradigm shift which will change his moment to moment experience for the better. The easiest way to do this is for him to enquire into the nature of life which entails investigating experience itself:

1. Consider the following statement: 'Life, for each of us, is just a series of moment-to-moment experiences'. These experiences start when we are born and continue until we die, rushing headlong after each other, so that they seem to merge into a whole that we call 'my life'. However, if we stop to look we can readily see that, for each of us, every moment is just an experience.

2. Any moment of experience has only three elements: thoughts (including all mental images), sensations (everything sensed by the body and its sense organs) and awareness of these thoughts and sensations. Emotions and feelings are a combination of thought and sensation.

3. Thoughts and sensations are ephemeral, that is they come and go, and are objects, i.e. 'things' that are perceived.

4. Awareness is the constant subject, the 'perceiver' of thoughts and sensations and that which is always present. Even during sleep there is awareness of dreams and of the quality of that sleep; and there is also awareness of sensations; if a sensation becomes strong enough, such as a sound or uncomfortable sensation, one will wake up.

5. All thoughts and sensations appear in awareness, exist in awareness, and subside back into awareness. Before any particular thought or sensation there is effortless awareness of 'what is': the sum of all thoughts and sensations occurring at any given instant. During the thought or sensation in question there is effortless awareness of it within 'what is'. Then when it has gone there is still effortless awareness of 'what is'.

6. So the body/mind is experienced as a flow of ephemeral objects appearing in this awareness, the ever present subject. For each of us any external object or thing is experienced as a combination of thought and sensation, i.e. you may see it, touch it, know what it is called, and so on. The point is that for us to be

aware of anything, real or imaginary, requires thought about and/or sensation of that thing and it is awareness of these thoughts and sensations that constitutes our experience.

7. Therefore this awareness is the constant substratum in which all things appear to arise, exist and subside. In addition, all living things rely on awareness of their environment to exist and their behaviour is directly affected by this. At the level of living cells and above this is self-evident, but it has been shown that even electrons change their behaviour when (aware of) being observed! Thus this awareness exists at a deeper level than body/mind (and matter/energy[49]) and *we are this awareness*!

8. This does not mean that at a surface level we are not the mind and body, for they arise in, are perceived by and subside back into awareness, which is the deepest and most fundamental level of our being. However, if we choose to identify with this deepest level – awareness – (the perceiver) rather than the surface level, mind/body (the perceived), then thoughts and sensations are seen for what they truly are, just ephemeral objects which come and go, leaving awareness itself totally unaffected.[50]

---

[49] The theory of relativity, and string theory, show that matter and energy are synonymous.
[50] C. Drake, *Beyond the Separate Self*, 2009, Halifax, p.18-20.

The Practical Application of Awakening

When one identifies with awareness each moment is encountered freshly and directly, uncoloured by past experiences. Most of our mental suffering and frustration is caused by our mind judging our experience as unsatisfactory, or by projecting into the future and worrying about the imaginary problems that this might hold. Whereas, from the viewpoint of awareness itself each moment is enough (in itself) as awareness does not judge but just witnesses 'what is'.

With this outlook one is much more capable of handling what the world may throw at us, as each moment is taken as it comes without relating it to the past, future or any imaginary self-image based on identifying with thoughts and sensations (mind/body). This does not imply that life will be without problems just that we will become more able to solve these as they arise.

With regard to solving these problems we have at our disposal the most amazing instrument, the human mind, our own inbuilt onboard computer. This is a wonderful problem solving device, but to function properly it needs to be supplied with accurate data. All computer errors are due to incorrect data or program bugs. The main program bug in the mind occurs when we identify

The Practical Application of Awakening

ourselves as the mind. In this case it colours all of the data it receives with its own opinions, judgements, self-interests and so on, which naturally leads to erroneous conclusions. As we learn to identify with the deeper level of pure awareness, this bug is fixed, and we learn to see things 'as they are', rather than through the filter of the mind. Now data is fed in uncontaminated, and problem-solving activity continues more accurately and spontaneously.[51]

So when one is 'awake' each moment is encountered freshly and responded to (rather than reacted to) appropriately, which enhances our problem-solving ability, thus making life easier and more enjoyable.

---

[51] C. Drake, *Beyond the Separate Self,* 2009, Halifax, p.92

Chapter Twenty Two

Love – Agape and Eros

This chapter discusses the differences between individual love, which is that exhibited by the 'separate being', and universal love, which is that exhibited by those who have realized that all beings are of the same 'essence'.

Love – Agape and Eros

This chapter considers the differences and similarities between two types of committed love, Eros that of the 'particular' for the 'particular' and Agape that of the 'universal' for the 'universal'. It will achieve this by considering the case for and against the proposition that they are completely different. It will attempt to show that the main difference in how we exhibit love boils down, once again, to identification: who or what we consider ourselves to be. This approach is particularly useful as it initially clearly defines the differences between Eros and Agape and then goes on to show how going beyond identifying as a separate being leads from the former to the latter.

In order to tease out the relevant arguments for and against the proposition that 'Agape and Eros are completely different' we will need to come to a clear understanding of what this actually means by defining, and fill out the meanings of, the terms Agape and Eros . However, before we can effectively understand their meanings we need a definition of love of which they are two different forms. Also it will be necessary to decide whether Agape actually exists or if it is 'logically empty' as the answer to this question will have a major influence on the debate.

Love – Agape and Eros

To define love is incredibly difficult as all of the definitions given tend to be of one of its various forms. Take for example the definition in the Australian Pocket Oxford Dictionary: 'Deep affection or fondness, sexual passion, sexual relations, delight in, admire, greatly cherish, like very much , greatly enjoy'[52] which gives a wide range of types of love. Generally there are considered to be six main forms of love. These are 'storge' which is a quiet and friendly attachment, 'eros' which is passionate and committed, 'ludus' which is playful and not committed, 'mania' which is obsessive and over-committed, 'agape' which is universal and altruistic, and finally 'pragma' which is practical in the sense of looking for a partner with the right qualities for a compatible relationship.[53]

The challenge is to find an overall definition of (the noun) love to which we can apply all of the above adjectives to show its different forms. Taking all of this into account, and bearing in mind that what we are discussing here is love between people (rather than the love of a good book, for example) I am going to define love as 'empathetic attraction' (for or to). Then the various

---

[52] *Australian Pocket Oxford Dictionary*, 2002, S. Melbourne p.647
[53] V.C. Demunck., *Romantic Love and Sexual Behaviour* 1998, Westport CT, p.37-38

Love – Agape and Eros

adjectives, associated with different types, will indicate its nature in terms of strength, commitment, attachment, etc.

Now we are in a position to attempt definitions of Agape and Eros, starting with the former which is defined in the AOD as 'Christian Love [Greek: Brotherly love]'.[54] This gives us the clue that we cannot conduct this discussion without recognising the central position occupied by Christianity and God in the debate. For the Christians were the ones who championed the idea of Agape as being the purest form of love:

> The classical understanding of love, expressed in the Platonic concept of EROS, was opposed in the Christian community by the biblical understanding of love, AGAPE ... which was translated into Latin as Caritas and appears in English as 'charity' and later, love[55].

This is also shown by the fact that the Greek New Testament only uses the word Agape and not Eros. So although philosophers generally like to keep such nebulous concepts as God out of their debates this will not be possible, in this particular case, as can

---

[54] *Australian Pocket Oxford Dictionary*, 2002, S. Melbourne p.20
[55] *Encyclopaedia Britannica* CD 99

also be seen from the Encyclopaedia Britannica definition of Agape: 'The fatherly love of God for man and man for God, necessarily extending to the love of one' s fellow man.'[56]

This love of one's fellow man is a very particular type of love in which: 'Thou shalt love they neighbour as thyself'[57]. The Christian is also exhorted to love his enemies and loving these combined, neighbours and enemies, amounts to loving all of one's fellow men equally regardless of one's relation to them. The 'as thyself' also shows that Christians are to love every person as if they were that person, i.e. they are to consider the wants and needs of others in exactly the same way as their own wants and needs giving them exactly the same weight!

There is also a non-religious version of Agape, for the statement just given is almost an exact definition of 'preference utilitarianism' in which one should always act in such a way as to satisfy the most preferences (wants and needs) of those, affected by one's actions, giving one's own preferences no greater weight than those of others.

---

[56] Ibid
[57] Matthew 22 : 39 *Good News, New Testament* Ingleburn 199

Love – Agape and Eros

This love is also natural to those who are identified with the deeper level of their being, pure awareness. For in this all people are seen to be of the same essence and equally valuable instruments of the Totality of consciousness and energy, which is the Absolute. Moreover, one is not identified as being a separate being which considers its own wants and needs to be more important than those of (seeming) others.

However, Christian (and nondual) Agape can go beyond preference utilitarianism to exhibit true altruism in which one does not consider oneself at all, such that love is 'sincere in its self-abnegation, a necessity of love'.[58] Thus Agape is a universal form of love in which one loves every person 'as thyself' and is always prepared, if the occasion demands it, to put others first.

Moving on to Eros which is more difficult to define, being much more than its AOD definition 'earthly sexual love' or 'urge towards self-preservation and sexual pleasure'. Eros was, in Greek religion, the god of love being the son of Aphrodite the goddess of sexual love and beauty.[59] Thus Eros is as much to do with love of beauty as with its derivative - erotic love. Plato, who

---

[58] S. Kierkegaard,, *Works of Love*, 1946, Oxford p.4
[59] *Encyclopaedia Britannica* CD 99

Love – Agape and Eros

believed the world to be based on archetypal forms, regarded Eros, in its highest form, to be a reaching out to ultimate knowledge (God) through the love of beauty:

> Complete initiation begins with the love of a single admirable body, continues with the realization that the beauty of an individual is paralleled by that of other individuals and goes on to esteem the beauty of the soul more highly than that of the body, thus rising by successive stages to ultimate knowledge, the culmination of which is the revelation of immaterial, divine and eternal beauty, in a word, God.[60]

Thus true Platonic love, which is a form of Eros, is an ascent of the soul through love of beauty to the highest Good, the Absolute Reality. 'Falling in love' with a single beautiful person can be the first rung on the ladder through which 'sense experience can suggest the Form of Beauty'.[61] Even much later Christian writers such as Anders Nygren have elaborated on this idea by saying that Eros is man's way to God through his own effort and is an upward movement towards God.[62] So Eros is a love with an

---

[60] R. Flaceliere, *Love in Ancient Greece*, 1960, London p.150
[61] *Encyclopaedia Britannica* CD 99
[62] A. Soble *Eros, Agape and Philia* 1989, St Paul Minn., p.94

Love – Agape and Eros

attachment for the beloved, be it human or God, with a longing to attain the beloved.

Before we can consider whether the Agape and Eros are 'completely different' we have to decide whether Agape actually exists, or whether it is logically empty. If it is logically empty this implies that it does not exist and thus we are unable to consider whether Agape and Eros are actually different in form. For difference implies having two forms to compare, but if Agape doesn't exist we are only left with Eros and you cannot compare something with itself. One could argue about the differences in the concepts of Agape and Eros but this would be comparing one actual form with another imagined form. From this we could draw the conclusion that they are completely different as you cannot have a much more 'complete' difference than between existence and non-existence!

Aristotle certainly maintained that Agape 'is not only impracticable but logically empty'[63] when he said:

---

[63] *Internet Encyclopaedia of Philosophy*, 'Eros', www.iep.utm.edu/l/love

> 'One cannot be a friend to many people in the sense of having friendship of the perfect type with them, just as one cannot be in love with many people at once (for love is a sort of excess of feeling, and it is the nature of such only to be felt towards one person)'.[64]

Here, however, I would disagree with Aristotle on both counts. Firstly I will attempt to show that one can be friendly with everyone that one encounters i.e. have true brotherly love towards all, and secondly that the love that he is describing is pure Eros which is only one form of love.

If we return to my minimalistic definition of love as 'empathetic attraction' we find that this means being attracted to someone with whom we can identify and so 'fully comprehend'.[65] This gives the clue that to attain brotherly love we must be able to identify with everyone we encounter. To do this we must be able to view every person as of the same essence and thus realize that there is essentially no difference between oneself and anyone else. In this case we can fully comprehend the essence of what it is to

---

[64] *Ibid*
[65] *Australian Pocket Oxford Dictionary*, 2002, S. Melbourne p.359

be human without needing to fully comprehend everyone's individual character traits.

In Christian terms this means to realize that we are all essentially souls beloved equally by God, for 'before God all souls are of equal worth', as Kierkegaard says: 'Your neighbour is your equal ... for with your neighbour you have human equality before God ... but every man has this equality and has it unconditionally.'[66]

Thus when one realizes that all others are essentially souls equally beloved by God one can truly identify with all and have love, or empathetic attraction, for them all. This is true Agape in Christian terms where one's love mirrors 'God's love for man' as one loves others as souls (made in God's image) of equal worth.

In non-Christian and nondual terms it is entirely possible to attain this same love by identifying oneself as an expression of cosmic (universal) energy and consciousness. In this view the universe is just a manifestation of this same cosmic energy, and consciousness, of which all life forms are expressions, using their minds and senses to experience and interact with the creation. Accordingly all members of the same species are of equal value

---

[66] S. Kierkegaard, *Works of Love*, 1946, Oxford, p.XI

and worth, and there is no *essential* difference between any of them. Then one can truly have the same friendly regard for everyone one encounters.

In both cases Agape is not possible if one is identified as a separate individual ego, for then one identifies others as such and the differences between egos are so great that one cannot truly 'identify with' all other's egos. As far as Aristotle's second point is concerned this is obviously Eros for he talks of 'being in love' and 'excess of feeling'.

So having posited that Agape is not logically empty and having defined Agape and Eros we can finally consider the proposition that 'Agape and Eros are completely different'. I shall first consider the case for the proposition that they are completely different:

If we start with the very origin of Eros, Greek mythology, he was said to have a brother 'Anteros, the god of mutual love, who was sometimes described as his opponent'[67]. This shows that the idea of Eros - passionate love - and Anteros (or Agape) - mutual (or brotherly) love - have been in opposition since their derivation.

---

[67] *Encyclopaedia Britannica* CD 99

Love – Agape and Eros

To highlight the differences I will comment and enlarge on those given by Anders Nygen in his seminal work 'Agape and Eros'[68] and then add a few of my own:

(a) 'Eros is acquisitive and longing. Agape is sacrificial giving.' Eros longs to acquire the beloved whether it be human or Godly, whereas Agape has no such agenda and reacts spontaneously and sympathetically as required.

(b) 'Eros is an upward movement. Agape comes down.' In Platonic/Christian terms Eros is an upward movement from man to God whereas Agape is God's love flowing downward or man loving in the same way as God.

(c) 'Eros is man's effort, Agape is God's grace.' Eros is an effort by man to obtain the beloved whereas Agape is a spontaneous outpouring requiring no effort and seeking nothing.

(d) 'Eros is egocentric, a form of self assertion… Agape is unselfish … it gives itself away.' Eros is based on identification as a separate individual ego seeking to obtain the other, whereas Agape is based on there being no essential difference between oneself and another self and thus occurs spontaneously seeking nothing in return.

---

[68] A. Sobel *Eros, Agape and Philia* 1989, St Paul Minn., p.94

(e) 'Eros seeks to gain its life, a life divine. Agape dares to lose it.' When identified as a separate individual self one can attempt to use love, as Eros, to gain union with God. However, when one dares to lose identification as a separate individual ego-self but identifies with the Totality (or as an equal soul made in the image of God) then Agape is a natural by product of this.

(f) 'Eros is primarily man's love; the beloved is the object of Eros. Agape is primarily God's love; God is Agape.' Eros is the love of the particular ego-self for the particular beloved, be it a human or God. Universal (or God's) love can only occur when man is not identified as a distinct, separate ego.

(g) 'Eros is determined by the quality, the beauty and worth of its object, whereas Agape is spontaneous and directed at all irrespective of any perceived beauty or worth.' Agape loves all equally without discrimination.

I do not quite agree with his final point, not given here, which I will change to:

(h) 'Eros recognises value in its object - and loves it. Agape loves equally recognising all to be of equal worth.' So Eros love an object because it values it, whereas Agape has no such ulterior motive.

Love – Agape and Eros

Finally I would like to add:

(i) 'Eros desires to attain a goal, be it the beloved or God, whereas Agape has no goal or motive.' Eros strives to attain union with the beloved or god whereas Agape does not strive at all having nothing to achieve or attain.

(j) 'Eros only occurs in intimate relationships whereas Agape can occur in all relationships.' Eros is normally a one-to-one affair whereas true Agape can occur in all of one's dealing with one's fellow man.

Summing up, given these ten major differences in which Eros and Agape are in almost direct opposition, one could maintain that 'Eros and Agape are completely different'.

Now to give the case against this proposition:

Some academics consider that there is very little difference between Agape and Eros, in fact J.A. Lee even goes so far as to say 'Agape combines aspects of Eros and storge.'[69] Indeed it is true that they do have some similar aspects for they are both forms of love, 'empathetic attraction' as I defined it earlier.

---

[69] V.C.. Demunck, *Romantic Love and Sexual Behaviou* 1998, Westport CT,, p38

Love – Agape and Eros

However, although there are many differences, as listed in the case for the proposition (all of which I consider to be valid), can we truly say that Agape and Eros are *completely* different? In fact can we say that any two things in existence are *completely* different? Consider a lamington and a super-nova, for example, they are both just different forms (or 'strings') of universal energy. It is true that they differ greatly in many aspects but they are both composed of the same 'essence'. In fact, as I said earlier, the only things that are *completely* different are where one exists and the other is non-existent. For in this case they are not even composed of the same essence, for one has no essence at all!

In this way it is very easy to see that Agape and Eros are not *completely* different but merely varying forms of the same essence, love. Eros being empathetic attraction of an individual for an individual, and Agape being empathetic attraction of the universal (or an individual identified with the universal) for the universal.

The differences in form, listed previously, occur due to differences in self-identification. For when one is identified as a separate individual one sees others as such and can only love on a one-to-one basis as one cannot truly empathise (i.e. identify) with all others. However, when one is identified with the Universal, or as a soul beloved by God of equal worth with all other souls , one can love universally as one can identify with (the essence of) everyone one meets. I will denote such a person as a '*universal being*' whilst denote one identified with the ego-self as a '*separate being*'. So if we scan quickly through the ten differences given previously:

(a) 'Eros is acquisitive, Agape is giving'. The *separate being* is always striving to acquire, the *universal being* knows that joy lies in 'giving and not receiving'.

(b) 'Eros is an upward movement. Agape comes down.' Eros can be directed upward as a way to achieve union. The *universal being* is already united.

(c) 'Eros is man's effort, Agape is God's grace.' The *separate being* is always striving, the *universal being*, through grace, knows there is nothing else to attain and exhibits Agape naturally.

(d) 'Eros is ego-centric, Agape is unselfish'. The *separate being* is identified with the ego; the *universal being* is unselfish knowing that there is, in reality, no separate individual ego-self.

(e) 'Eros seeks to gain a life divine, Agape dares to lose it.' The *separate being* seeks to gain divine life for itself.

The *universal being* dares to lose itself (identification as a separate individual) completely.

(f) 'Eros is man's love, Agape is God's love'. Eros is the love exhibited by a separate ego-self, Agape is the love exhibited by God, or the Universal totality of Being, or those identified as such.

(g) 'Eros is determined by beauty and worth, it is 'motivated', Agape is 'spontaneous' 'overflowing'' The *separate being* is striving to gain something beautiful or of worth, the *universal being* knows that there is, in truth, nothing more of worth to gain and overflows with love for his fellow beings.

(h) 'Eros recognises value, Agape loves equally.' The *separate being* loves the beloved for its value; the *universal being* has no judgement of value and does not discriminate between his fellow beings.

(i) 'Eros desires to attain a goal, whereas Agape does not.' The *separate being* is always striving to attain a goal, better himself etc., whereas the *universal being* knows there is nothing more to attain.

(j) 'Eros occurs in intimate relationships, Agape can occur in all'. The *separate being* can only love on a one-to-one basis whereas the *universal being* loves all.

So it can be readily seen that the differences are mainly based on self-identification; and that, as Agape and Eros are just different forms of love, they cannot be said to be 'completely different'.

Appendix One

So What ... What Now?

This chapter from *Beyond the Separate Self* concerns how to establish one's awakening whilst living in the world. It also highlights some of the wonderful outcomes of awakening which make day to day existence easier and more joyful.

So What ... What Now?

If you have got this far you will, I hope, have experienced the peace provided by truly knowing that beyond the mind/body there is a deeper level of pure awareness. However, you could say 'So what?' for we have to live in a body in the physical world with all of its associated problems. The trick here is to learn to live from this deeper level of awareness whilst negotiating living in the world. This has five major components, the first of which is primary, and if completely adhered to takes care of the following four:

1. Be committed to completely identifying with the deeper level of pure awareness, for in this there is always perfect peace and repose. Before this complete identification with pure awareness is established one will flip/flop between identifying with awareness and identifying with a mind/body. Awakening is an ongoing process with complete identification with pure awareness as the final goal. For it is in fact a series of awakenings, which is very necessary due to our natural tendency to go back to sleep! Every time we 'flop' back to identifying ourselves as mind/body we have nodded off again; and so the 'flip' to identifying with the deeper level of our being is another awakening. The author knows this only too well, and makes no claim to 'lack of sleep'.

So What ... What Now?

As one investigates and cultivates this deeper level, the periods of 'wakefulness' are prolonged and consequently one 'nods off' less. The period of time between one's first awakening and being completely awake is indeterminate and varies greatly from being to being. However, this is not a problem, for as the periods of 'wakefulness' (which are totally carefree) increase so will the commitment to identifying with the level of pure awareness. This will lead to more reflection and investigation, resulting in further awakenings which will continue the process. To call it a process may seem a misnomer for when one is 'awake' there's no process going on, but the continual naps keep the whole thing running.

This commitment to identifying with the level of pure awareness involves having faith in our body/mind to negotiate living in the world, for this is what it has evolved to do. This 'complete identification' will not happen all at once but is something that has to be cultivated. I would recommend doing this by spending three periods of at least twenty minutes, every day, totally relaxing into the recognition of pure awareness. The best times for this are between getting up and engaging in one's daily activities, after the day's work is over and just before going to sleep. The first 'sets one up' for the day, the second refreshes and re-energises one after the day's toil, and the third aids in achieving a deep and peaceful night's sleep. One may argue that there is not enough time available for this, but these meditations provide so much relaxation and recharging that one can easily recover the time by sleeping for an hour less.

When meditating/contemplating, the body needs to be completely at ease, so pick the most comfortable position you can find. For instance, the final session can be carried out lying flat on your back just before dropping off to sleep. There should be no distractions, but if there are any just notice them as ephemeral objects that come and go in the constant conscious subjective presence that underlies all thought and sensations. You may use any of the preceding chapters as aids to your relaxation and investigation into the recognition of pure awareness.

As time goes by you will make your own discoveries and verbalize your own pathways into this recognition. I strongly advise you to record in writing these discoveries and pathways, as the reading of them before your practice will put you in the right frame of mind, and inspire you. In the final analysis your 'pathway in' will become particular to your own mind, and writings produced by your mind will always appeal more than

So What ... What Now?

those produced by another mind. Ultimately you have to become, as the Buddha said, 'a light unto yourself'.

2. To avoid identifying with your thoughts and mental states, you need to stay alert so that you are not carried away by negative (or any) mind-states. For a stream of thoughts and mind-states continues to come up whatever your degree of realization; however, as complete identification with pure awareness is cultivated, this stream will diminish. The point is to recognize these thoughts and mind-states for what they are: ephemeral objects which come and go quite naturally, leaving the constant conscious subject untouched. It is important not to identify with them (as mine or me) and thus give them extra weight. To avoid this, practice treating them as entertainment and either thank the mind for bringing them up, or examine them as strange phenomena. As your realization deepens, this will happen spontaneously and no effort will be required.

3. Learn to trust the mind/body. The body functions quite naturally without much mental intervention being necessary. We do need to feed and clothe it, but apart from that it functions quite happily, provided we are alert to the signals that it emits such as hunger, thirst, tiredness, inertia, etc. As far as solving the

problems involved in living in the physical world are concerned, we have at our disposal the most amazing instrument, the human mind, our own inbuilt onboard computer. As previously said, this is a wonderful problem solving device, but to function properly it needs to be supplied with accurate data. All computer errors are due to incorrect data or program bugs. The main program bug in the mind occurs when we identify ourselves as the mind. In this case it colours all of the data it receives with its own opinions, judgements, self-interests and so on, which naturally leads to erroneous conclusions. As we learn to identify with the deeper level of pure awareness, this bug is fixed, and we learn to see things 'as they are', rather than through the filter of the mind. Now data is fed in uncontaminated, and problem-solving activity continues more accurately and spontaneously.

4. Accept 'what is' with no resistance, for resisting what is here and now only causes suffering. Such thoughts as 'I wish this wasn't the case' or 'If only… then this wouldn't have happened' cannot possibly change what is 'here and now', and only lead to dissatisfaction and anxiety. If such thoughts do come just let them come and go without buying into them, by either regarding them as entertainment or thanking the mind for them. This does not mean that we cannot or should not plan to change things in

the future for the better or so that we do not find our selves in the same situation again. It is self-evident, however, that we are powerless to change 'what is' as it already is!

This also means accepting our mistakes and not berating ourselves for them, for until we are totally identified with, and as, pure awareness, we will continue to make mistakes. Normal life is a mixture of correct decisions and mistakes and should be accepted as such. As we become more 'awake' we will make less mistakes, but until then we can always see any annoyance caused by our errors for what it is: just a mixture of fleeting thoughts and sensations. Once again, if one relaxes into the deeper level of pure awareness one will see that this is totally unaffected by anything occurring at the surface level of mind/body. At this deeper level each moment is enough, or perfect in itself, as awareness just witnesses 'what is' without ever seeking to change anything.

5. Live totally in the present moment with no regard to the past or future. This naturally occurs once one begins to live by following the previous components. Then thoughts about the past and future will be seen for what they are, ephemeral objects which come and go. Also the stream of thoughts and mental

states will decrease and thus the mind will experience longer periods of stillness. When this occurs one sees things 'as they are' in reality, and this combined with acceptance of 'what is' leads to the mind's preferences and judgements losing their power. This does not mean that you will have no preferences, but that you will remain unaffected if they are not satisfied. One of the easiest ways to bring oneself into the present moment is to completely focus on the bodily sensations and see them as they are with no judgement and without reading any non-specific meaning into them.

One of the major pitfalls of the mind is to read meaning into things that have no meaning. All superstition and much of religion is based on this, and when this occurs it takes one away from experiencing what is 'here and now'. This is a classic case of the mind creating imaginary problems which it then attempts to solve. At first one will find that present moment awareness is only a fleeting state that comes and goes, but the more you completely identify with pure awareness the more this state comes, and remains, and the less it goes.

When there is this complete identification (merging with awareness) one discovers that it has many wonderful by-products, most of which are considered to be spiritual disciplines in the mystical paths of the world's religions. However, practising these disciplines to achieve self-realization is an example of putting the cart before the horse, for the recognition of oneself as pure awareness is primary and these disciplines are secondary outcomes of this. Some of these wonderful by-products are as follows:

Compassion

Once one sees that at the deepest level one is pure awareness, it follows that this is known to be the case for all sentient beings. At this level there is truly no separation between oneself and any other being, and this naturally leads to compassion.

Discrimination between the 'real' and the 'unreal'

This level of pure awareness is classified as the 'real'; it is constant, unchanging and unaffected by any 'thing', whereas the level of manifestation of things is classified as 'unreal', it is always changing and is governed by the laws of cause and effect. Once one becomes completely identified with pure awareness then this becomes obvious and no discrimination is needed.

So What ... What Now?

Love of God and one's fellow man

The word God means consciousness having two states: at rest (pure awareness), and in motion (manifestation). In this there is truly no separation as the essence and ground of all that exists is consciousness, and true love is only present where there is no separation; true love is 'no separation'. The Christian idea that 'God is Love' points to this, and love of one's fellow man naturally follows from the realization of no separation.

Contentment and remaining unaffected by external circumstances

Pure awareness is always unaffected by external circumstances, thus complete identification with awareness naturally leads to this quality of being.

Detachment

Pure awareness is always complete in itself and prefers no 'thing' or circumstance, being the witness to these. Therefore detachment is its natural condition. This does not mean that we will have no preferences at the level of mind/body, just that we will remain unaffected if these are not fulfilled as there will be no attachment or clinging to them.

Therefore in this complete identification with pure awareness one is totally beyond the 'separate self', for even as it continues to rear its ugly head one does not buy into or identify with it. There is also no more existential anxiety or mind-induced suffering. This is not to say that mental and physical pain will not occur – these are an unavoidable facts of bodily existence – but they will not produce mental suffering for they will be seen for what they are, ephemeral states which come and go. Even in the case of prolonged physical pain it is possible to accept this without resistance, so that although there is pain this does not cause mental suffering. Also, in this complete identification one can always sink into the deeper level of pure awareness where there is only peace and tranquillity.[70]

---

[70] C. Drake, *Beyond the Separate Self*, 2009, Halifax, p.89-96

Appendix Two

All or Nothing

A discussion from *Beyond the Separate Self* about the importance of committing to identifying with the deeper level of awareness if one wishes to overcome anxiety and mental suffering.

All or Nothing

At this point you may say 'Well that's all very well but what about *me* and *my* story?' For it has long been held by Western psychology that the sum of one's experiences and conditioning makes up what one *is*. This may well be true at the surface level of mind/body, but not at the deeper level of pure awareness in which these experiences come and go leaving no lasting impression. It is the surface level that is the domain of the 'separate self', the ego, and this is where anxiety and mental suffering occurs.

At this stage one needs to come to a decision about which one values more: the objective level of thoughts/sensations or the deeper subjective peaceful level of pure awareness. If one chooses the former then life will just continue with its highs and lows, suffering and anxiety, and obsession with the 'separate self'. One will also continue to see everything through the distorting filter of the mind, its opinions, judgements and self-interest, which lessens one's perceptions as if seeing through a darkened window. However, if one chooses the latter then all perceptions are heightened by seeing things clearly, 'as they are', for when nature is seen 'as it is' it is much brighter, more vivid, more stunning than when seen through the mind's filter. So by identifying with pure awareness the objective level of sensations is enhanced, and thus becomes more valuable in its own right. This gives the lie to the idea that sinking into the deeper level of being means that one enjoys the world less; in fact the reverse is true!

It may be true that one can continue to value the surface level of thoughts/sensations more, and occasionally sink into the deeper level of pure awareness for a brief respite from the troubles of daily life. However this does not tap the full potential of identifying with, and as, this deeper level completely beyond the 'separate self', and experiencing things 'as they are' in their absolute immediacy and totality. In this mode there is no concern for the future, and the past completely loses its hold, thus all worrying comes to an end. For this to occur one has to completely let go of 'my story' and see everything in the past for what it is, totally gone and in the past.

This is truly a case of *all or nothing*, for once any exception is made then this is the thin end of the wedge as it sets a precedent for other past experiences to be held on to. It has to be completely realized that nothing that has happened in the past or will happen in the future can possibly affect the deeper level of pure awareness.

All or Nothing

I have heard from many people who, having glimpsed this deeper level, continue to argue for the value of 'working through past experiences', and in this they are dishonouring that which they have glimpsed. For the only way that you can completely work through past experiences is to totally let them go, and not buy into them when they reoccur in the mind or body. They will continue to come up, but any attention that is lavished on them only feeds and strengthens them; when ignored they are starved of attention and their reoccurrences will slowly peter out. By 'ignored' this do not mean 'suppressed', for this will also strengthen them, but just allowed to 'come and go' with no weight being given to them.

As soon as you start telling yourself a story about what they mean, or how they have affected you, you are back at the surface level of the 'separate self' and the ego. If the physical feelings are too strong to ignore they can be defused by going completely into them without any 'story', and noticing that they are just sensations which have arisen and will subside quite naturally. It is the telling of the story that prolongs them, feeds them and invites them to reoccur.

All or Nothing

However, even these unpleasant memories/feelings point directly to pure awareness for this is where they occur and are noticed by the mind. This brings up a very important point: any time where there is any mental suffering caused by identifying with painful thoughts, or feelings, this should be a wake-up call to the fact that we are misidentifying. Any mental suffering can be used as a direct pointer back to the deeper level of our being: pure awareness.

So to fully tap the potential of this deeper level one needs to fully commit to identifying with, and as, this. This commitment is paramount, for, as previously pointed out, one will continue to flip/flop between identifying with the deeper and surface levels of our being. As we have spent so many years identifying with the mind/body, we will naturally tend to do this, so we need to continually bring our attention back to the deeper level and to commit to doing this.

In the final analysis the surface level is the abode of the 'separate self', ego, with all of its attendant self-obsession and suffering. The only way to go totally beyond this is to dive deeper than this and discover 'the peace that passeth all understanding' of pure

All or Nothing

awareness. This, however, will not totally inform and transform one's life until one totally commits and identifies with this.[71]

---

[71] C. Drake, *Beyond the Separate Self*, 2009, Halifax, p.97-101

The Author – A short spiritual biography

I was born into a strict, but joyful, Methodist family. From the ages of 11-17 I was sent to a Methodist boarding school, which I left with the conviction that organized Christianity was not for me. I could see that what Christ said about living was wonderful, but that the church did not really promote his teachings rather concentrating on him as our 'saviour' and on the purportedly 'miraculous' facets of his life. It was also very apparent that many so called Christians were not interested in practicing what he taught. This was now 1965 and living in central London during the years of flower-power I experimented with various hallucinogens, finding them very beneficial for opening my subconscious which allowed years of conditioning to pour out. This left me feeling totally 'cleansed' and unburdened, ready to start life anew in a spirit of investigation as to the nature of reality. The psychedelic states also presaged, gave a glimpse of, mystical states which I suspected were attainable through spiritual practices. I then embarked on a study of Gurdjieff and Ouspensky which I found absolutely fascinating and was convinced that self-realization was the purpose of life. However, they made the process sound so onerous that (being young, foot-loose and fancy-free) I decided to shelve the whole project temporarily.

It was not until eight years later that I resumed the spiritual search when Janet (my partner) introduced me to my first yoga-teacher, Matthew O'Malveny, who inspired us by quoting passages from the Upanishads, Dhammapada, and other scriptures during the class. He also emphasized the importance of relaxation and meditation. There followed a few years of investigating various spiritual paths including a prolonged dalliance with the Brahma Kumaris (Raja Yoga) whose meditations were wonderful, but whose dogma was very hard to take. We then moved into the country to start a pottery and immersed ourselves in Satyananda Yoga, an organization which had no dogma but taught a wide range of yogic practices. We were both initiated into *karma sannyas* by Swami Satyananda and adopted a yogic lifestyle consisting of asanas, pranayama, yoga nidra, meditation, kirtan and vegetarianism.

During this time I was at a silent retreat when I happened to pick up a volume entitled *The Gospel of Ramakrishna* which introduced me to this amazing being who practiced many spiritual paths, within Hinduism and also Islam and Christianity, discovering that they all lead to the same result. He was then approached by many devotees from these various paths all of whom he was able to teach in their own path, whilst emphasizing the harmony of religions. A few years later I was lucky enough to find an erudite nun in the Sarada Ramakrishna Order, based in Sydney, who initiated me into the worship of this amazing being. This entailed two to three hours of daily meditation, *japa* (mantra repetition) during daily activities, reading every word said by or written about him, including daily readings of *The Gospel of Sri Ramakrishna*, and chanting. I continued this sadhana quite happily for ten years.

I then encountered a disciple of Sri Ramana Maharshi, Gangaji, who said 'Stop! Be still, you are already That'. The message being that the effort and search were masking that which is always present; all that was required was to 'stop' and see what is always here. After many years of struggle and effort this news came like a breath of fresh air and I glimpsed the essence, that undeniable ever-present reality. This was followed by a seven day silent retreat which resulted in my first 'awakening', and also in an ecstasy that slowly faded over the following year.

My first book *Beyond the Separate Self, The End of Anxiety and Mental Suffering* came about from the realization that occurred then and has matured over the following 12 years. During this time I wrote a series of articles, for an e-mail news group, based on my meditations and contemplations, around which that book is based. At the same time I have also completed an honours degree in comparative religion and philosophy, using the insights gained by my spiritual practices to inform my essays. Some of these essays were adapted to include as chapters in that book.

My honours thesis, together with an essay about Ramakrishna used to highlight the themes explored, has now also been published by www.nonduality.com under the title: *Humanity, Our Place in the Universe, The Central Beliefs of the World's Religions.*

Glossary

Advaita: non-dual.

Brahman: the all-pervading transcendental Absolute Reality.

Dharmakaya: the Absolute Unmanifest Reality that is 'Aware Nothingness'.

Dvaita: dualist school of Vedantic philosophy proposed by Madhva.

Ein sof (or *En-Sof*): the infinite nothingness, the source and final resting place of all things.

Fana: absorption into the Absolute, which al-Junaid of Baghdad interpreted as 'dying to self'.

Kali: the Divine Mother, creator, preserver and destroyer. Sakti, cosmic energy, consciousness in motion.

Lila: the divine play or manifestation, consciousness in motion.

Maya: the power of Brahman, which supports the cosmic illusion of the One appearing as the many.

Nirmanakaya: the dimension of ceaseless manifestation, or the compassionate energy of Rigpa.

Nirvana: Buddhist word for *moksa*, enlightenment, awakening.

Nitya: the Ultimate Reality, the eternal Absolute.

Om: Brahman 'The Impersonal Absolute'; but is also the Logos, The Word, in the 'Ground of Being', in which all manifestation arises, exists and subsides.

Plenum: a space filled with matter, or the whole of space so regarded (OED).

Rigpa: pure awareness which is 'the nature of everything'.

Sakti: cosmic energy, consciousness in motion.

Samsara: the wheel of birth, life, death and rebirth.

Sefirot: the stages of divine being and aspects of divine personality.

Siva: universal consciousness when it is at rest, aware of every movement occurring in it, which is 'pure awareness'.

Sunyata: the void, formless awareness, aware nothingness.

INDEX

A

A Course in Miracles, 38
Absolute, 36, 66, 145, 160. *see also* Brahman
acceptance, 148, 197–198
ACIM (A Course in Miracles), 38
advaita vedanta, 50, 123–125
agape. *see* love
anxiety, 53, 57, 63, 95, 107, 112, 144, 202. *see also* suffering
Aristotle, 181–182, 184
atman, 50, 124
attention, on awareness, 64
authority, no outside, 43
awakening, 48
   as realization, 78–82
awareness, 31, 53–55, 144
   and the Absolute, 36
   all things as pointers to, 100
   attention on, 64
   being aware of, 38, 97–101
   and body/mind, 122–123
   and brain, 84–87
   and choicelessness, 108–109
   committment to, 193–196, 204, 207–208
   and compassion, 200
   as consciousness, 134–136
   and detachment, 201–202
   and effort, 108
   as factor for enlightenment, 38
   identification and, 5, 24
   investigation of, 107–110
   as limitless, 35
   as love, 39
   nature of, 26–27
   as omnipotence, 35
   as omnipresence, 34, 109
   as omniscience, 34
   as pure, 35
   qualities listed, 34–36

as radiant, 110–111
as the real, 200
and restless mind, 59–61
as stillness, 33, 61, 93
as subject, 91
as substratum, 32, 92
as This, 36
and thought, compared to, 97–98
and thoughts and sensations, 91–92
as universal consciousness, 32–33
as what we are, 87, 132

B
Barnes, Hazel, 131
body/mind, 32, 48, 48–50, 56, 92, 122–123, 132, 135, 140, 163, 196–197
boredom, 94
Brahman, 50, 124, 127–132. *see also* Absolute
Brahman, 147
brain, awareness and, 84–87
Buddha, 38, 42, 97, 105
Buddhism, 117, 123

C
Camus, Albert, 137, 141–142
choicelessness, awareness and, 108–109
Christianity, 42, 79–80, 115–116, 123, 177–179, 183
compassion, 200
computer, mind as a, 22–23
consciousness, 33, 34. *see also* awareness
    as awareness, 134–136
    as container, 136
    as field of energy, 133–134
    play of, 70
    universal, 32–33
Course in Miracles, 38

D
Descartes, 43
detachment, 201–202
direct experience, 99

Divine Mother, 129
doing nothing, 54
dream, as separate objects, 48

E
effort, awareness and, 108, 146
Einstein, 133
email address of Colin Drake, 20
energy, field of, 133–134
energy, universe as, 41–42, 75–76
enlightenment, 38, 145
   seven factors of, 97
eros. *see* love
essence, 160–166
existentialism, 160
experience, nature of, 31, 48, 90–91
experiential vs intellectual recognition of truth, 107, 111
experiments to investigate awareness, 107–110

F
fear, 46. *see also* anxiety, suffering
free will, 160–166

G
God, 38, 39, 42, 160, 177–178, 180, 201

H
Hakuin (Song of Freedom), 103–105
Hinduism, 116–117, 127

I
identifying, 45
   with awareness, 5, 24
illusion, 69
inquiry, 43, 48, 49, 63
intellectual vs experiential recognition of truth, 107, 111
investigating nature of reality, 30, 33, 36, 38, 40–41, 43, 51, 55, 57, 79–81, 90, 95, 97, 100, 107–112, 121, 133
Islam, 116, 123

J
Jesus, 38
Jnana, 98
journaling, encouragement of, 6
Judaism, 115, 123
Jung, Carl, 136–137

K
Katha Upanishad, 50, 124
Kena Upanishad, 50
Kierkegaard, Soren, 183

L
Lee, J.A., 187
light, awareness as, 110–111
light, unto self, 42
lila, 70, 129–130
love, 39, 42
    agape and eros as different, 185–187
    agape and eros as not different, 188–191
    agape defined, 177, 178
    definitions, various, 176
    eros defined, 179–181

M
Maha Sattipatthana Sutta, 38, 97
Mahayana School, 102
mantra meditation, 64–66
meaning, 129–132, 151–155, 155–158
meditation, 195
    as artificial, 61–62
    mantra, 64–66
    Nisargadatta Maharaj on, 64
    as restless, 59–60
memory, 68–70
mind, 69–70
    as a computer, 22–23
    as danger to being aware of awareness, 99

nature of, 26, 27–28
restless, 59–60
as servant, 61
mind/body. *see* body/mind
(the) moment, 90, 93–95, 138, 142, 149, 198–199

N

Nisargadatta Maharaj, and mantra (quoted), 64
non-separation, 42, 46
nonduality, 73–76, 103, 114
nothing exists, 146
nothing, meaning of, 155–158
nothing to do, 54
nothingness, 64–66, 68
(the) now, 146. *see* (the) moment
Nygren, Anders, 180, 185

O

omnipotence, awareness and, 35
omnipresence, awareness and, 34, 109
omniscience, awareness and, 34

P

play of consciousness, 70, 129–130
purpose, 129–132

R

radiance, awareness as, 110–111
Ramakrishna, Sri, 100
reality, 112. *see also* awareness; investigating nature of reality
realization, 107, 111
recognition of thought, 60–61
religion. *see* individual religions
Rigpa, 87

S

Sahaj Samadhi, 103
Sartre, Jean Paul, 160
Schopenhauer, 141

search, spiritual, 144
Secret, The, limitation of the movie, 90
'seeing', 7
seeing of thoughts, 60–61
Self, 50. *see also* awareness, Brahman
self-image, 46, 130, 139
self-improvement, 46
self-inquiry, 43, 48, 49, 63
Self-nature, 103, 112
self-realization, 107
sensations. *see* mind/body; thoughts and sensations
separation, 45
Sheldrake, Rupert, 137
singularity, 127
Sogyal Rinpoche, 87
Song of Freedom (Hakuin), 103–105
spiritual search, 144
stillness, 33, 34, 35, 75–76, 109–110
string theory, 133–134
subject, awareness as, 91
substratum, awareness as, 32, 92
suffering, 9, 23, 45, 105, 139. *see also* anxiety
Svetasvetara Upanishad, 51

T

Taittiriya Upanishad, 127–128
Tao, the, 97
Taylor, Richard, 131
The Meaning of Life, 131
The Secret, limitation of the movie, 90
things, meaning of, 151–155
This, awareness as, 36
thoughts and sensations, 136, 144. *see also* body/mind
 awareness and, 91–92
 compared to awareness, 97–98
 and effort, 108
 as element of experience, 91
 as ephemeral, 91, 93, 144
 identification with, avoiding, 196
 seeing of, 60–61
Tibetan Book of the Dead, The, 55–56

totality, 136–142
truth, 105. *see also* awareness

U
unified field theory, 133
universal consciousness, 32–33
universe, as energy, 41–42
Upanishads
   Katha, 50, 124
   Kena, 50
   Svetasvetara, 51
   Taittiriya, 127–128
   various, 123–125

V
Vaishnavism, 123
Vedanta, 114, 162–163

W
what is, 91–92, 147
witness, 50–51

Bibliography

Australian Oxford Pocket Dictionary 2002, Oxford University Press, S. Melbourne

Conze, E., *Buddhist Scriptures*, 1959, Penguin, Harmondsworth.

Drake C., *Beyond The Separate Self,* 2009, Nonduality Publications, Halifax

Drake C., *Humanity Our Place in the Universe,* 2010, Nonduality Publications, Halifax

De Munck V.C. *Romantic Love and Sexual Behaviour* 1998 Praeger, Westport Ct.

Easwaran, E., The *Upanishads*, 1988, Penguin, New Delhi

Encyclopaedia Britannica 1999 on CD

Flaceliere R. *Love in Ancient Greece*, 1960, Frederick Muller, London

Good News New Testament 1999 Australian Bible Society, Ingleburn' Vic.

Internet Encyclopaedia of Philosophy, www.iep.utm.edu/l/love

Kierkegaard S., *Works of Love* 1946, Oxford University Press, London

Nikhilananda, S., *The Gospel of Ramakrishna*, 1942, Ramakrishna Math, Chenai

Nisargadatta Maharaj, *I Am That*, 1997, Acorn, Durham NY

Padmasambhava, *The Tibetan Book of the Dead*, trans. by Gyurme Dorje, 2005, Penguin, London

Prahbavananda, Sw., *The Upanishads*, 1986, Ramakrishna Math, Myalpore

http://nisargadatta.co.cc/pages/quotes_consciousness_and_absolute.html